**Publications of the
American Folklore Society**

New Series
General Editor, Patrick B. Mullen

Miles of Smiles, Years of Struggle

Stories of Black
Pullman Porters

■

Jack Santino

University of Illinois Press

Urbana and Chicago

This book is printed on acid-free paper.

Library of Congress Cataloging-in-Publication Data

Santino, Jack.
    Miles of smiles, years of struggle : stories of Black Pullman
porters / Jack Santino.
        p.   cm.
    Bibliography: p.
    Includes index.
    ISBN 0-252-01591-6 (alk. paper)
    1. Brotherhood of Sleeping Car Porters—History. 2. Trade-
unions—United States—Afro-American membership—History.
3. Discrimination in employment—United States—History.
4. Race discrimination—United States—History.   I. Title.
HD6515.R36S26 1989
331.88'1138522'0—dc19   88-20981
                                                                    CIP

In memory of my father, John F. Santino

Contents

Preface

This book began with a public program at the Smithsonian Institution in Washington, D.C. It was decided to feature a panel of retired Pullman porters in a workshop at the 1978 Festival of American Folklife, in order to note the merging of the Brotherhood of Sleeping Car Porters (BSCP), the first successful black labor union, with a larger union, which effectively marked its passing. At the Smithsonian, we wanted to draw attention to its importance. As the folklorist in charge of this program, I interviewed dozens of retired porters in the Washington area. Many were too old to travel or too sick to take part in the museum program, although they were able to talk to me and allowed me to record their words. Many of the most interesting, most dedicated, most important men had passed away, it seemed. Yet, as time wore on, men who were still strong and articulate, and generous with their time, emerged. Several porters agreed to contribute to the program and appear in person at the National Museum of American History to tell their stories and answer the questions of the public. Acting as a liaison, I tried to elicit those stories and anecdotes about life on the railroad that I knew were interesting and representative of the particular nature of the porter's experience. I try to do the same herein. (For a fuller account of the circumstances of the collection of these narratives, see the Appendix.)

Following the Smithsonian program in 1978, the project grew as I began to develop ideas of doing an ethnographic documentary film with Paul R. Wagner, a filmmaker I knew and had worked with previously. I was awarded a grant from the D.C. Community Humanities Council, administered through the Columbia Historical Society, in 1980, to carry out the project, which resulted in the film, *Miles of Smiles, Years of Struggle: The Untold Story of the Black Pullman Porter*, Benchmark Films, 1982. In the course of working on the film, I met and interviewed porters such as E. D. Nixon, of Montgomery, Alabama, the man who organized the 1955 bus boycott that brought Martin Luther King, Jr., into the civil rights movement, and C. L. Dellums, one of the original founding officers of the BSCP and uncle of Congressman Ronald Dellums of Berkeley, California. I also met a truly remarkable individual, Mrs. Rosina Coruthers Tucker. Born in 1881, Mrs. Tucker is the widow of a porter and an activist herself: former president of the Ladies Auxiliary to the BSCP and former international secretary-treasurer of that group, Mrs. Tucker held secret union meetings in her home, lodged A. Philip Randolph when he came to Washington, and secretly disseminated union literature.

All these individuals will make their presence felt throughout this book, as will many other rank-and-file workers who were willing to share their memories, stories, life histories, thoughts, and beliefs with me. Foremost among equals here are Mr. Lawrence W. (Happy) Davis, Mr. Leroy C. Richie, Mr. William D. Miller, Mr. Green Glenn, Mr. Ernest Ford, Jr., Mr. Homer Glenn, Mr. Walter C. (King) Cole, and Mr. Rex Stewart. To all of them, my sincere and deepest gratitude, and my hope that I have done justice to the story of their lives.

I would like to thank Roger D. Abrahams, Richard Bauman, Marilyn Ferris Motz, and Patrick B. Mullen for having read part or all of this manuscript and for making many helpful suggestions. Samuel Brylawski, Recorded Sound Division, Library of Congress, helped me locate many film and music references. Judith McCulloh was encouraging and patient throughout the development of the manuscript, and Beth Bower was a skilled and enthusiastic editor. To all of the above, I extend thanks and appreciation. Finally, I would like to thank my wife, Lucy M. Long, for her encouragement and her faith in me. I could not have written this book without her.

■ Introduction

Pullman porters lived and worked in an era of American history that stretches from the Civil War to the conflict in Vietnam. As black workers serving a rich white clientele, they came to symbolize a golden age of rail transportation. In the 1920s, while images in books, movies, and popular songs were defining them as grinning, shuffling servants, Pullman porters organized what would become this country's first successful black labor union. From 1925 until 1937, porters withstood physical abuse, job insecurity, intimidation, and brute force to triumphantly assert their essential dignity and to claim their rights as human beings.

Porters worked: the story of Pullman porters must encompass more than the story of their union, the Brotherhood of Sleeping Car Porters, and their leader, A. Philip Randolph, because, as great as those stories are, the porter was above all else a working man. His work was and still is the center of his identity. The nature of the work was service, and although the service was complicated by racism, and the job was rooted in slavery, it was the only job available to him which paid better than unskilled labor. A Pullman porter worked in a segregated society under discriminatory job rules, often with racist passengers and racist conductors, but he also met good and caring passengers and conductors, and formed strong, almost familial bonds with those men he called his brothers.

Porters played: during layovers in Pullman quarters away from home, the porters spent long hours playing card games while talking, joking, and laughing with their comrades, and they caroused in the strange cities they stopped in. But porters also took action: in the 1920s and 1930s, when they could no longer tolerate the discrimination against them, a group of porters organized the Brotherhood of Sleeping Car Porters. The true story of the Pullman porter must encompass all aspects of his life: work and play, suffering and action.

In 1978, the Brotherhood of Sleeping Car Porters (BSCP) merged with a larger union, the Brotherhood of Railway and Airline Clerks. Superhighways and jet airliners had long since rendered the plush Pullman sleeping cars an anchronism; by 1967 the Pullman Company had become exclusively a manufacturer of railroad cars rather than a lessor of cars and personnel. Nor was it any longer a major passenger carrier. In 1979, A. Philip Randolph, leader of the BSCP and a major civil rights activist, died in his home in New York; the era of the Pullman porter was over. But the men still meet, even today.

Picture one such meeting of the Association of Retired Pullman Porters in 1981. It has just broken up on the south side of Chicago. Mr. Walter Cole is standing among a group of men. He is telling his friend, Mr. Rex Stewart, about the time the Pullman Company tried to buy off the leader of the porters' union, Mr. A. Philip Randolph. "They sent him a check for twenty-five thousand dollars. And he *refused* it. So they sent him a blank check. He could have written anything he wanted on that check; he could have had as much money as he wanted. But he sent it back to them. He said, 'You could buy my parents but you can't buy me.' And I love that man in his grave today." All the men know the story. They shout approval and encouragement as it is being told and as Mr. Cole adds his own personal commentary. Perhaps it is more accurate to say they are reliving rather than retelling the story.[1]

Mr. Cole and Mr. Stewart are retired Pullman porters. Mr. Cole was born on June 16, 1886, which made him 95 years old at the time. Mr. Stewart was 80. They, like the other men present, have spent their lives in service to the Pullman Company and its patrons, and as members of the Brotherhood of Sleeping Car Porters. Even though the union has effectively ceased to exist, men such as these— the porters who came from the cities and farms of America, who went to work for the industrial giant known as the Pullman Company and wore the coveted uniform of the Pullman porter—continue to meet, both formally and informally. They discuss issues of importance to their lives such as retirement benefits; they organize trips to hospitals to visit ailing friends; and they mourn the passing of a brother. And when the serious business is done, the meetings resound with the rich voices of old friends enjoying each other's company. Men gather into small groups to play the porters' own card game, bid whist, which they claim was invented by porters to help pass the long hours on layovers in strange cities between trips. And they tell stories, like the one about A. Philip Randolph and the blank check.

The Chicago meeting ends in late afternoon. The men are getting old; the job has changed (women and white men work as porters today on Amtrak), but originally it was a job for black men exclusively. Their cycle is ending, but in the earlier years of this century, Pullman porters were on the front lines of one of the most important social revolutions in this country's history. Their union proved that blacks could organize successfully and that blacks were not strikebreakers as they had usually been portrayed. It forced the American Federation of Labor to grant a charter to a black union, thus breaking down institutionalized racism in organized labor; it donated funds and lent considerable expertise to the civil rights movement; and it allowed black people a degree of economic security they had not known before.

The Chicago scene is repeated in cities all over the country. Porters regularly gather, years after their retirement, to play cards or go to the racetrack. Every city with a railroad station has a community of porters who are members of a fraternity that stretches across the United States and into Canada—wherever the tracks went. Their bonds are racial, political, and social, but primarily occupational; their community and their identity have been formed by their years as Pullman porters and by the living and working through of the unique paradoxes of that job. They are an occupational community, and this is the study of the occupational folklore of a contemporary group of special men.

Occupation is at the base of their brotherhood and fraternity, but occupation must be understood to encompass the totality of the porters' experience. The work itself (making beds, cleaning cuspidors, attending passengers, and so on); the discriminatory job rules (P.M. time, running in charge, doubling out, and more); the routine racism, as well as the tipping, the fun, the struggle to unionize—all of these contribute to the porter's occupational identity; they form his personal and cultural history. This book is about the making and establishing of personal identity in an occupational setting through personal experience narrative and, to a lesser extent, other expressive forms of occupational lore, such as jokes and legends. That the occupation of porter was a service one is a crucial factor, as is the fact that its workers were black men. The porters' stories are derived out of their effort to maintain their dignity under an onslaught of contradictory demands, pressures, beliefs, and symbols. Throughout this volume, their narratives are seen as artistic, social, and cultural creations, oral artifacts that are used by porters to recreate the past in a way that is meaningful to them today, that helps them to establish who they are and why things were the way they were.

This book contains the porters' own understanding of their past and of their occupational lives. As such it presents a kind of folk history. I am interested in the perspectives of the porters regarding their media image, unionization, the early years of the Pullman Company, and the role of porters within those early years. The data enrich the scholarly discourse on Pullman porters by adding the porters' own descriptions of their culture to the data historians have provided. Much of the material throughout the book consists of narratives that are stylized and performed (orally) as such. We cannot always take the stories at face value. Many are legendary in nature, such as the story of A. Philip Randolph and the blank check. The fact that the story exists does not prove that a blank check ever existed. On the other hand, the fact that this legend can be found in many variants does not prove that an attempt to bribe Randolph never occurred. Rather, these narratives should be approached as cultural products, not necessarily as factual accounts per se. They must be read with the goal of learning about the way the expressive culture of porters—their folk sayings, jokes, stories, and games—reflects and reveals their perception of their situation. In chapters 3 and 4, I examine the ways they used storytelling strategically to cope with their situation; in chapter 5, their pictures of themselves, as revealed in their traditions, are contrasted with their media images.

The stories and testimony of this book are viewed within the context of the lives of the individual porters, the occupational experiences they have had, and the social climate in which they lived (one of segregation and routine racism), as well as in the context of unionization and organization as a response to job inequities. Not all the porters' words are taken from storytelling sessions. I do use their descriptions and reports of their lives as firsthand accounts of historical contexts, especially in chapters 1 and 2. More often, however, their testimonies represent the incorporation of real events into their own experience and the reshaping and transformation of these events into narratives which express and embody central concerns and values; this process is the mark of a good storyteller.

Not surprisingly, there are traditional stories that the porters circulate that are also found in variants. Moreover, personal anecdotes tend to be clustered around shared occupational experiences: porters swap stories about passengers, conductors, tips, and so forth. Very often, these stories are traditional in the strict sense that they are told by several porters and known to many more; in the larger sense, these stories come out of, and speak to, the occupational experience. The performances are traditional in terms of the occasions, settings, and style of the telling,[2] and they are traditional in the sense that they focus on points of shared experience and commonality and therefore are mechanisms for identifying occupational relationships and maintaining group membership. They are products of the occupational life; they are narratives that are the results of the process that Dell Hymes has called "traditionalizing experience." [3]

The recounted historical events happened to these men and because of these men, and the past is recreated in anecdotes that are specific to the individual porter and to the porters as a group. A. Philip Randolph and the Brotherhood of Sleeping Car Porters have been studied in other important volumes,[4] but this book marks the first time a significant body of stories, reminiscences, and oral history has been collected from the black men who worked as Pullman porters in America and been added to available resources. On one level, we are finding out more about the men themselves, what they saw, what they say, feel, and think, because these men are important. We are also interested in the way culture works, and these porters provide a case study of an occupational group engaged in a service job featuring conflicting demands of status and complicated by racism deeply rooted in American culture.

NOTES

1. Walter "King" Cole, May 18, 1980.

2. Sandra Stahl, "The Personal Narrative as Folklore," *Journal of the Folklore Institute* 14, nos. 1–2 (1977): 9–30.

3. Dell Hymes, "Folklore's Nature and the Sun's Myth," *Journal of American Folklore* 88 (1975): 345–69.

4. See, for instance, Jervis Anderson, *A. Philip Randolph: A Biographical Portrait* (New York: Harcourt Brace and Jovanovich, 1973); Brailsford Brazeal, *The Brotherhood of Sleeping Car Porters: Its Origin and Development* (New York: Harper and Brothers, 1946); William Harris, *Keeping the Faith: A. Philip Randolph, Milton P. Webster, and the Brotherhood of Sleeping Car Porters 1925–1937* (Urbana: University of Illinois Press, 1977).

1. The Historic Setting

The story starts in slavery, and slavery is the context of all that will follow. In the first years after the Civil War, when George Pullman was developing and refining his plush sleeping car service, he used ex-slaves to serve as porters, and today the porters remember their history as having begun as a continuation of the slavery the war supposedly ended: "When we first started to work, we were slaves for the Pullman Company. You see, we were slaves ... we made the Pullman Company," as one porter stated succinctly.[1]

In 1869, the railroad was the fastest, most efficient way to travel long distances, but not the most comfortable. Tracks had been laid across the entire country, so transcontinental rail travel was now a reality, but George Pullman saw that it was at the same time "a nightmare."[2] It was not his original idea to build sleeping cars—they had been available since at least 1830—but it was George Pullman who had the business acumen to realize that if he were to offer especially comfortable, even luxurious, sleepers, the large passenger market would be his.

Pullman was born to God-fearing, industrious parents in New York state in 1831. He moved to Chicago in 1855 and experimented in many fields until he got involved with railroad cars. Aiming toward the development of a "hotel on wheels,"[3] Pullman experimented with his earliest sleepers in 1860. The first ornate, luxurious car, the Pioneer, was built in 1864, and was used to carry the body of the assassinated President Lincoln from Chicago to Springfield, Illinois. By 1865, Pullman had persuaded the Michigan Central railroad to run his cars on its Detroit to Chicago line. Within three years he had incorporated his manufacturing and railroad leasing industry, known as the Pullman Palace Car Company, in Illinois and had extended his service to several railroad lines, offering Pullman passengers "through" service coast to coast. He retained ownership of his cars, leasing them to various railroads. Passengers bought tickets specifically for the Pullman cars, which had their own conductors to collect them in addition to the conductors for the regular train. Whereas the long-distance traveler on a regular train was required to change cars several times during a lengthy trip, a Pullman car went the entire trip on a series of railroads; the car, not the passenger, changed lines, which made cross-country travel much more attractive.[4] The passenger could board the Pullman and never have to switch later, because the cars were transferred from train to train.

Through the 1870s, Pullman went on to exceed all expectations of both the public and the business community. He built lounge cars, club cars, and dining cars; the sleepers were enlarged and improved. At the advent of transcontinental travel, George Pullman was a businessman in the right place at the right time with the right ideas. However, convenient and comfortable travel was not the entire reason for Pullman's appeal to the public. From the beginning, he was determined to offer much more than simply comfort: he would offer luxury. It would be more than the plush interiors of the cars; it would take the form of personalized service to the passenger.

New technological improvements in hardware and equipment helped to differentiate the Pullman Company's sleeping cars from the rest, but the crucial difference was the personal, human service Pullman provided each customer on every trip. Early on, as he began to expand his operations, he realized that were he to hire a force of workers whose job would be one of total personal attention to the passenger, he could offer the public an original, unique, and superior overnight travel service. After one or two faltering attempts to utilize conductors, and then women, to provide this personal service, Pullman turned to a largely untapped labor force in need of employment. In large numbers, recently freed slaves were hired.[5]

The porters' duties were several and servile. Pullman seemed to think that former slaves would more readily perform the often distasteful chores such as cleaning cuspidors, or at least be less likely to balk at them. Black men, from their point of view, saw the Pullman Company as a way up and a way out of poverty. Many men say it was "the only game in town," and it was a relatively prestigious game. As one porter remembers it, "It was a good job for a black man. In 1915 Pullman employed more blacks than anyone else. He was responsible for black migration North. Most of today's professional black men probably spent some time on the railroad."[6] As we shall see, the porters today are neither uniformly positive nor uniformly negative about their job experiences. There are aspects of it they valued, just as there are aspects they despised. And while not all of today's black professionals spent time on the railroad, it is not uncommon to find that a parent, uncle, or grand-parent did. The Pullman Company was the largest private employer of black labor in the country by the 1920s, and this large-scale hiring contributed directly to the creation of a black middle class later in the century.[7]

Service was the essential job duty of the porter, and service was the primary selling point to the passenger. The porter became the living symbol of the Pullman Company and the occupational figure most closely associated with, and representative of, a golden age of rail transportation in the United States. To whites, the porter represented service and luxury; to blacks, he represented status and mobility, both physical and social. One porter phrases it this way: "I used to wave at the white-suited porters when the train ran through, and I left South Carolina to get one of those jobs. Neckties were mandatory, and you have to understand, blacks were *elated* to get out of denims."[8] Denims were field clothes, work clothes that reminded the men of slavery; the clean, crisp uniforms of the Pullman porters were seen as genuine status symbols, a major advance. Men were elated to get out of denims, to get out of the field (where they picked cotton), because this reminded them of a past in which they had been bought and sold.

Slavery is the holocaust of American blacks, and like the Holocaust, firsthand experience of it is not needed in order to despise and reject it. The porters I interviewed did not experience slavery firsthand, certainly. The oldest man whose testimony appears in this book was born in 1881. Others, men in their eighties and nineties, were born closer to the turn of the twentieth century, but even these men did not entirely escape the sting of human bondage. For instance, porter Leon Long, ninety years old at the time of this writing, remembers his youth spent on the edge of slavery:

> My father was old enough, his parents were slaves, and he was practically a slave. They lived on a farm down there in Jonesville, North Carolina. I can remember, everything we wanted, we had to go up to the "big house," as they called it. I remember that. He was on the *edge* of it. It was practically slavery in a manner of speaking. Everything you wanted you had to go to the big house and speak to the boss. If they wanted to use a team to go to town to get themselves something or other, to eat, well, they had to go up to the big house.[9]

Porters remember their history as beginning in slavery, or being derived out of it. It underlies all else that will follow in this book:

the ways porters feel about the service they performed, the tips they earned, the conductors they worked with, and the abuse they took. Although the story they tell is not entirely ugly—they had many great times and good memories—they see things in terms of slavery, and it is important to understand that. For instance, Mr. C. L. Dellums, although a few years younger than Mr. Long, makes it a point to establish that he is a generation closer to the slave experience than most men alive today. He says,

> Yes, my father was actually born in slavery. Now, generally, January 1, was looked upon, you know, as the liberation of the slaves. But there wasn't slave one freed January 1, 1863, not one. Abraham Lincoln's proclamation didn't free anybody. Slaves weren't free in Texas until June 19, 1865, and my dad was born in April, 1865. So he was a slave baby, you know, for about two and a half months. So when I say I'm the son of a slave, I am the son of a slave. And then I was born only thirty-five years later. So, you see, I was born pretty close to slavery myself. And conditions in this country, well, I would have changed it for anybody's country then, if I could, because conditions were damned bad. My mother worried herself sick, worrying over me. She fought with my father; she'd wake me up sometimes way in the night with a big loud talking row, and I learned she was telling him that I would never live to get grown, and she blamed him because he wasn't teaching me to how to get along with white people, and one night he finally told her, "Who in the hell is going to tell white people how to get along with *him*?" So I grew up under bad conditions—poor, limited as to where Negroes could live in a small town. It's amazing that any of us lived to get grown.[10]

Mr. Dellums begins his story, and the porters' history, in slavery.[11] Although we are not yet dealing with the tales and legends of the job, we are seeing the way these people, under these conditions, in a certain time and place, choose (consciously or unconsciously) to remember aspects of their past, and how they use it to make sense of the present. Their emphasis on slavery, and their appreciation of the importance of uniforms as status symbols, indicate that race and social class were important factors in the formations of their identities, both personal and communal. Scholars recognize the concept of multiple group identity; that is, we all are members of groups whose identity is derived from region, family, ethnicity, occupation, religion, and so forth.[12] Depending on the context of the social situation, one or more of these will be fore-grounded, but the others remain as dynamic aspects of an individual's sense of self. In the case of the porters, occupation dominates as a primary agent in their sense of both personal and social identity. Perhaps this is because race, social status, and economic status were each collapsed in the job. To say you were a Pullman porter was to say that you had a job that paid well compared to other kinds of work available to black men; it meant you were able to qualify for the position and thus had no police record and were both intelligent and trustworthy; it meant you were a black male who worked as a servant to the wealthy and powerful individuals who rode the Pullmans. To be a Pullman porter was for many an all-encompassing identity.

The concept of slavery that informs the porters' ideas about their job is complex: the first porters were drawn from the ranks of slaves, and many porters were born to slave families after slavery itself had been abolished; in a more figurative sense, they were economic "slaves" to the Pullman Company, paid lower wages than whites for comparable work, and forced (in part by the tipping system) to act like slaves to their passengers. Moreover, racism and segregation were society-wide. The black man working on the railroad might find himself unable, for instance, to buy lunch while on a stopover in a small town. From Mr. A. C. Speight we hear of the following such incident:

> Yeah, we had difficulties everywhere. . . . You talk about your Boston, you could find a whole lot of difficulties right there. Well, I didn't have what you might call difficulties, but I had—a bus came by and a youngster yelled "Hey, nigger!" Course, I cussed him out. You had difficulties in Canada. We went to Canada (I took my wife on a trip) and the man wouldn't serve me a beer—in the bar, in Canada, now. So, you had difficulties just about everywhere. Let's go back to Las Vegas. I went in there to eat. I had plenty of money in my pocket. Well, I didn't have plenty—I had enough. So, she says to me, "We don't feed your kind in here. We don't feed your kind in here." So, we had to wait until we got up to . . . the [national] park up there, and they wouldn't feed us, and this was government land. So, the boss told them, "These people are on government land. You better feed them."[13]

This from Hunter Johnson:

Right here in Ohio, I got off the train. I walked up the street
and met an old white fellow. I said, "Mister, where can a
man get a good hot meal?" He turned around and he spit—
all his moustache was yellow from tobacco. He said, "Well,
there ain't nowhere for a darkie to eat around here." That's
in Ohio. So I had my little sterno stove in my bag. I went
back there and warmed up some ham, fried me an egg, and
toasted bread in my little pan and I sat down, hot water,
made me some coffee, and I did just as fine as going to some
lunchroom, although I had to cook it and serve myself. I had
money in my pocket and couldn't buy food.[14]

Many porters tell stories of such occurrences, and they are
often quite similar in detail. Mr. Rex Stewart of Chicago, for instance, tells the following:

Here's what happened to me one time when I first went
to Rochester, Minneapolis. I went uptown to get my
breakfast, so I walked into a little restaurant and the girl
came over and gave me a set-up—silver and a glass—and she
said to me, "The boss would like to see you." So I stepped
toward the kitchen and he told me, "I can't feed you in
here. But I can feed you on the chopping block." I said, "No
thank you." I gave the girl fifty cents and thanked her for
the set-up. I smiled and went on out. So I went over to a
little grocery store and got me some stuff and went over to
the car and ate it.

That night, this guy and his daughter were on their way
to Chicago, and he came down to the station, and I smiled
and I looked at them. He was so ashamed. He turned all red
in the face. I told him, "That's all right."[15]

In his telling of this incident, Mr. Stewart is careful to show
that he never lost face; at no point did he surrender his dignity.
He never gave in to anger, always remained composed, smiled as
he left the restaurant, and forgave the owner when he met him at
the station. The railroad was Stewart's territory; even though he
was a porter, he was in charge of the social situation when he met
the restaurateur. Now he was in control, and he chose to exercise
that power graciously.

This anecdote points to some of the basic dichotomies of the
porters' job: they worked in a racist society (notice that the porters
are insistent that the problems did not exist solely in the South,
but also in supposedly unlikely places such as Boston, Canada, and

Ohio); they dealt with their passengers from the low-status position of a service worker; they had to please these passengers in order to get the tips they depended on—but they were also hosts on the train. They had a kind of power and control over the traveling public that, because of the ambiguous nature of their position and the ambivalent attitudes of the public toward them, they had to be very careful in displaying.

Ernest Ford, Jr., describes another time when porters could not eat because the restaurants would not serve black men. Often in situations such as this, porters simply bought provisions at a grocery store and prepared their own meals. In this case, however, all the stores were closed, and it appeared that the porters might not eat at all. The conductor of the train (for the railroad, not the Pullman conductor) sided with the porters, Ford recalls: "I hauled soldiers also in a seventeen-car train, and we stopped to let the soldiers eat in a town down in Natchez, Mississippi, and all the soldiers got off. They were waiting and ready to feed them when we got there, right ahead. It was on Sunday and all the stores was closed up, and the conductor decided that he wouldn't move the train until they would let us eat. And finally they agreed."[16]

This is a brief little reminiscence, but the fact that the porters were not going to be fed until an authoritative white man insisted they be is, upon reflection, rather startling. Because these experiences were common, these anecdotes and narratives based on personal experience tend to be paralleled from porter to porter. Leon Long talks of a similar occurrence, trying to find lunch in a small and segregated town. This should suggest the abundance of such stories, and, by implication, the routine racism of a society in which black people in general did their best to live and work.

> Now we were down in St. Petersburg. There was a convention of some kind down there. Now there was no place you could go in and order a meal, there were no places down there. There were just a few places that anybody could eat at that time, few cafes, didn't amount to anything much. Well, the conductor would have to up and find a place that we could go into and get something to eat at, and make arrangements, and they thought that was a big deal. The man came back and said, "I found a place. Come on, I'll go with you." And we went in. Usually we went in the *back* door, and he took us right through the *front* door, and he said, "Go right on through." We walked right on through until we walked through to the *back yard.* He had a

big thing for a table like a *stump* that somebody'd clean fish
on, took an old linen bag over the thing, it smelled like fish.
They put us right out in the sunshine! Sun shining right
down on us. We couldn't go into a place down there and get
nothing to eat. Our money couldn't be spent down there.
And we were there for five days![17]

The Pullman Company hired blacks for a relatively well-pay-
ing job, but at the same time, Pullman institutionalized inequity
and discrimination in many of its rules and regulations. So a young
black man in the early years of this century was locked into a
frustrating and particular set of circumstances in which most of
society's prestigious paths were closed to him, many of its institutions actively hostile, while others, although they shared in the
general social evil, at least had something to offer to black men.
The Pullman Company was not altruistic; it was pragmatic. Black
labor sold Pullman: the service that the porters rendered was the
single most important selling point for the Pullman Company. It
was in the company's interest to hire blacks as service employees.
The black man, for his part, saw the job as an opportunity to travel
and a chance to earn money.

Those who did were inspirations to their families. For instance,
Ronald Dellums, a U.S. congressman from Berkeley, California, tells
a family legend about his uncle, C. L. Dellums, one of the founding
members of the Brotherhood of Sleeping Car Porters. But, first, we
have the words of C. L. himself, which bear witness to the plight
of the bright, ambitious black man in the early years of this century,
and the needs and impulses that led him away from home and,
finding all other doors closed to him, to the Pullman Company:

I started work for the Pullman Company in January of 1924.
I got fired for my union activities around the first of October
1927. So, I didn't have a very long career with the Pullman
Company, and of course I didn't intend to. I still had hopes
on becoming a lawyer, and I was seeking work to get my
law degree at the University of California. But racial
discrimination was rampant in the big districts then and
there was no way for a Negro to get a decent job in the early
'20s. I went to work for the Pullman Company as a last
resort of trying to find work, still hoping to go to law
school.[18]

Congressman Ronald Dellums:

When he came to California he said, "I don't plan to wear these overalls for the rest of my life," and he chose to train himself. As a kid, I felt that was a very powerful statement, a very strong statement about a human being who could overcome odds on his own. That was a very powerful thing to me, it had a tremendous impact on me personally.

One of the things that was most impressive to me as a kid was a story that my parents told that C. L. Dellums was a self-taught person who came to California from Corsicana, Texas, who bought dusty old books and taught himself. Everyone that I met as I grew up thought that C. L. had a number of degrees from major universities around the country. This articulate, eloquent, knowledgeable person— there's no way he can not be a university graduate from one of the Ivy League colleges. Everybody thought this. And that gave me even greater pride, that I knew he hadn't gone to college, that he taught himself.[19]

Although not every porter went on to enjoy the kind of successful accomplishments of C. L. Dellums, it is true that the men who became porters were admired by their friends and families for taking on the work, for the travel that the job involved, and because the money they earned allowed poor families to be self-sufficient. The social advancement of the porters allowed their children to go even further. To echo Mr. Ford, who says that most of today's professional black men probably spent some time on the railroad, we can say that a great many successful black professionals today are the sons and daughters, grandsons and granddaughters, nephews and nieces, of Pullman porters. Ronald Dellums is an outstanding but not atypical example.

A Pullman porter represented status, then, in terms of costume (professional uniform as opposed to laborer's denims); mobility (ability to range across the country as opposed to being rooted in one place); urbanity and sophistication as opposed to rural simplicity; and change as opposed to sameness. Even in terms of their musical tastes, porters were associated with the urbane jazz of the big cities rather than the rural blues and folk music of the country. Everything about the Pullman porters is consistent with this image of urbanity and sophistication. Just as they left their field clothes behind and eagerly adopted neckties and jackets, so they left field music behind and listened instead to Count Basie, Duke Ellington, Charlie Parker, and Billie Holliday. However, they affected traditional music and became agents of change by the nature of their work. Because they traveled to the large urban centers of the country, they had access to recordings of jazz and blues musicians from all areas of the country, many of whom were traditional, which they in turn brought back to rural towns. Many traditional musicians have testified that it was the Pullman porter who introduced them to certain pieces of music.[20] Moreover, porters traveled with musicians as passengers, and many porters learned to play from these professional jazz musicians, informally, while passing the long hours of the night around a piano. Meeting admired people was one of the attractions of the job, but on a different level, it is this mediation of rural and urban lifestyles that gave the porters special status in their communities. What the porters did in terms of music, they did in terms of the culture of their small or insular communities generally: they introduced some of the values and ideas of the mass society, in a gentle way, to the folks back home who wondered about such things from afar and from what they heard and saw in the media.

Most porters seem to have entered the occupation with the help of a relative. In some cases, working for the Pullman Company was almost a family tradition: porter Leon Long of Washington, D.C., belongs to such a family. His father was a porter, his uncle was a porter, his two brothers were both porters, and each of his two sisters married porters!

A porter who was a family man often had to sacrifice certain family pleasures because of the job. Porters commonly tell of having regularly missed Thanksgiving dinner, or Christmas, with their families. One man had to leave his daughter's wedding to go to work. The rewards of the job made it worthwhile, however, and family members admire their porter-husbands and porter-fathers. There is a persistent rumor about porters, that they had families "at both ends of the line"—that they were bigamists. Most porters deny the truth of this rumor by pointing out the impracticality of it. "I could barely take care of one family," says one man. "What would I want with two?" I have never met a porter who admits to having been involved in such an activity, and most find the suggestion offensive, although some men claim to know *other* men who did it. Whether there is any truth to the gossip, or whether it is simply and only rumor, no more and no less, is uncertain, but there is no reason to believe that if some men did engage in bigamy, they were more than a very few.

Despite their long absences from home, porters' families were usually happy families. The father had the respect and admiration of his children. Porters' wives talk about the long waits, never knowing when their husbands would return, but they were generally supportive, and in fact proud, of their spouses. Likewise their children: when Leon Long reminisces about his childhood, he remembers his father leaving in his white jacket and returning days, even weeks later, to entertain his children with stories of the things he had done and the places he had seen. Says Mr. Long:

> I was born in 1893. My father worked for the Pullman Company. He was working out of Asheville, North Carolina at that time. Then he moved down to Chattanooga, Tennessee. My older brother, he went into service, working for the Pullman Company. So my whole family, right on down the line, worked for the Pullman Company: my father, my older brother, then the brother younger than I. He was the next one to go with Pullman service. I went in after that. My two sisters, they married Pullman porters.
>
> My father used to tell us, talk about the trips. He'd talk about the scenery and the different places he'd been in. He didn't have a regular line all the time, and sometimes he'd get stuck on a sidetrack for three, four, maybe five days. Because he used to run down to New Orleans, out of Chattanooga, Tennessee. A lot of times he used to carry me down on the cars where he was working, while he was making down [the beds on the cars] and all that. Along them days, they had combs, brushes, for the passengers. So when they got up they didn't have to do nothing, because they had combs, whisk brooms during them days. He had to carry a lantern, and had to carry coal and make fires for some of them cars to keep them warm. That's *way* back then. Around 1909, back in them days. That's when I got interested in it. I thought that was great to see him leaving with his white coat on and all that stuff. That was out of Tennessee. . . .
>
> My father would tell us lots of stories, a lot of nice things and a lot of comical things. . . . He'd be all the time telling us something that happened on the train, on the trip. Some good, some bad, some funny. Some of the bad, what you would consider bad, be some kind of run-in with the passengers, people thinking they're better than you, and [calling you] Uncle Tom, boy, and George. Never call you by your name, and somebody come along "geeching" you in the side, to see you jump. I remember things he told us about the good passengers. Seemed like he was one of the porters

passengers took a liking to. One of the men hired him from the Pullman Company, hired him for his valet.

Most of his run-ins were with conductors. You know how some people think they own the whole world, and they want to push you around and put hardships on you and have you to do part of their work and all like that. Instead of them doing their own work, they'd push the work onto the porter. Along in them days I never heard him say he went too far to use any vulgar language or anything with them. Least little thing that happen in them times you'd have to go up on the carpet. They'd be pretty likely to give you a day off if you did anything. The least little thing you do, if you said any smart words or anything like that, well, they'd have you up on the carpet and lay you off for a trip or two. You couldn't stand up to them.[21]

Mr. Long is typical of porters when he takes care to point out that his father got along well with passengers, less well with conductors. As we will see later, porters tended to respect their passengers, but they had a great many conflicts with the Pullman conductors who worked the Pullman cars, and sometimes with the conductors employed by the railroad whose train was pulling the leased Pullmans.

It was common for a man to work with the Pullman Company and urge other members of his extended family to apply: a brother, a father, a brother-in-law, or even a cousin's husband, as in the case of L. C. Richie. Mr. Richie was born in North Carolina at the turn of the century, and was encouraged to apply to the Pullman Company for work. He did, and was hired on April 9, 1926. He moved to Pittsburgh in order to work and go to school, "though," as he says, "that was my last year in school." Lawrence W. Davis, known to his friends as "Happy" Davis, described his joining the Pullman Company in his typically jovial manner: "I began in 1925. The man told me, 'You won't see your family hardly ever.' I said, 'More power to it!' But it was a blind-alley job. You went there as a porter and you left there as a porter. There was no advancement." Finally, an even more serious view of this same phenomenon is expressed by Homer Glenn of New York. Mr. Glenn is quite eloquent in discussing the fact that economic conditions forced black men to become Pullman porters, and that in taking the job, one suffered losses of educational opportunities and family ties. These losses hurt very much, and it was questionable whether the job was worth the trade-off. When asked if he liked his job, Homer Glenn answered, "Yes and no."

I had six brothers, and my father was dead, and my mother was there, and she'd say to me quite a few times, I don't know what we're going to have for dinner. I don't have any money. And my brothers started to stay out, with the girls I guess, stay out all night, and don't bring any money home. And my mother was struggling, trying to make me stay in college. Finally, I decided that I had to quit. I didn't want to see her suffer. So, I came to the Pullman Company. Came out of school, started to work here. *No* is because I had the opportunity that I passed up. Being out here on the road, working as a Pullman porter and seeing the things that go on, I have sat right here on this seat and cried a many a night because I did not go to college and finish college. The opportunity was there, but it was hard, and I couldn't afford to see my mother suffer as she did. So this is why the answer is no.

Number two, the answer is yes. I like my job. I like it because I have no other alternative. I've always been taught if I'm going to do something, do it to the best of my ability. And I had no other place to go. Lost my school opportunity. And I had no other opportunity and no alternative but to stay as a Pullman porter. And I do like the job. When I started to work for the Pullman Company, I had no alternative—no other alternative. So when I found out I had no other alternative, I liked the job. Yes, I liked it. Had nowhere to go, nothing to do. And I made this my top priority—Pullman porter.[22]

At best, Mr. Glenn's testimony is ambivalent. He says he both liked and disliked the job, but he has a difficult time explaining why he liked it. Every positive statement is framed by a disclaimer: "When I found out I had no other alternative, I liked the job." This deep-seated ambivalence reflects the two dichotomized aspects of being a Pullman porter: it was a good job because it was available to blacks at a time when most other jobs of comparable stature were not, and because it paid well relative to those menial jobs that were. It was a bad job because it took the porters away from any other educational opportunities; it was a blind-alley job with no advancement (black men did not become conductors); and the service nature of the job reinforced certain social relationships of white superiority that had been institutionalized by slavery. Considering what they gave up, what did the porters get in return?

Although the Pullman Company hired large numbers of black people for the job of porter, it was a difficult job to get, considering the high unemployment and low job opportunities at the time. As such, the job conferred select status upon the porters in their communities. On the train, however, the porter was a servant. He quickly learned that conditions were unjust and that racial inferiority had been institutionalized by the Pullman Company in its job regulations. The porter was in the difficult position of having the duties of a host, but none of the rights.

Anthropologist Ralph Linton has described status as a collection of rights and duties,[23] and it is a condition of service occupations that the duties be foregrounded and emphasized so that attention is called to their performance, as when a flight attendant fluffs a passenger's pillow, a cab driver gets a passenger's bags, or a porter brushes a man with a whisk broom. Simultaneously, the concomitant rights are confused, sublimated, or nonexistent. Although a porter is in control of the situation vis-à-vis a passenger and functions as the host (and, in fact, often functions as a conductor under the practice of "running in charge"), in order to perform and project the role of servant, he must not be seen to have the rights that otherwise are afforded to a host. Thus we have the first set of contradictions, or paradoxes, of the porter's life and work: it was a good job and it was a bad job; he had the highest status in his community and the lowest status on the train; he must perform the duties of a host and behave as a servant. It was out of this contradictory situation that he developed his routines, his conventional ways of performing services for the customers.[24]

The Pullman Company exploited economic and racial conditions in America by offering black workers an alternative to field labor or unemployment that was, nevertheless, inequitable and demeaning. At a time when professional job opportunities for black males were virtually nonexistent, men were eager to go to work for Pullman. They found almost immediately that the job was not as attractive as it had appeared. Well into the 1930s, a porter was on call twenty-four hours a day. Any time a passenger rang, the porter had to respond. He had to be ready to awaken passengers in time for them to be ready to depart the train at their stop, and these stops occurred around the clock. Even after they were allowed a few hours sleep a night, porters slept on a couch in the smoking area of the men's room, while passengers would come and go to the toilet throughout the night.

Leon Long:

> We were entitled to four hours sleep a night, during the last part of when we were working, the later years. You

were working with the next man, the man next to you. So you go to bed, get your four hours first, and he looks out for your car whilst you get your four hours. See, I'd go to bed around ten o'clock and get up around two o'clock, and he is going to look out for my car, then I got to look out for his car until about six in the morning.

In the early days, conditions then were very bad. If you wasn't a regular porter—and even if you *were* a regular porter—you didn't have nowhere at all to sleep. You had a seat in the smoking room. If you got any sleep at all, that would be in the smoking room. And they'd put up a curtain between you and the lavatory, the toilet, and if you got any sleep at all, that's where you got your sleep. Sometimes if you were an extra man, the *older* man, the regular porter tells you he's going to get his sleep, and you got to kind of watch out for his car and yours, too. And then you sign out the passengers at the end of the line and go to the office and get signed out onto another run—you were the extra man— you don't get no sleep again. I remember I went to Nashville to Dallas, Texas, for three or four nights, and I was the extra man. They put on an extra car, so they say I don't get any sleep. So I had to set up and do the best I could. I *hopped*.

I had a car, an old folks car. The Spanish-American War Veterans had their convention in Dallas, Texas. I had a car, and they had one bed was supposed to be for me to sleep in. And we were gone for nine days. And the passengers that I had was old people and the place where I was supposed to sleep—that's where they put their baggage. I didn't have no place for nine days, and I liked to die.[25]

Fred Fair:

We had no sleep, certain runs. They give us three hours a night. Well, that's not much sleep for working all day and night. You'd have to work while the other man sleeps. You'd have to watch his car while he got three hours. And on certain runs, they didn't get *no* rest on it. There was a man from President Wilson's cabinet—I don't know if it was Baker or Hoover, but it was one of them—was running to Cincinnati one night, and when he went to bed, the porter was sitting in the smoker. And he got up during the night and went in the toilet, which was right there in the smoking room, and he saw the porter sitting there. He was there when he went to bed, and he was still sitting there. So, this man was coming back from Cincinnati the same night, so he caught the same porter back. The same thing happened. So he asked this porter if he didn't get any sleep. He said, no, he didn't get any sleep, he stayed up all night. As I say, he was in the cabinet there with Wilson, and he changed that. That's why we got the three hours out of the job. He didn't get any change until we got the Brotherhood. After that, they give us the three hours. But he went to somebody, I don't know what he did. I think his name was Baker.[26]

Homer Glenn remembers:

In the early days when we first came on we had one little bed on the couch in the smoking room—the smoking room is where we'd shine our shoes, mopped up the floor when people went to bed. We had to do that, and we had to wash out the cuspidors (there were cuspidors we had to clean out because you had to sleep there). And then by the time you get that halfway done and make your bed, somebody comes to the bathroom, and they'd slam the door and then would leave it open. So you get up to close the door, and you only had two and a half hours sleep. And all night long, the door is slammin,' the door is slammin.' In fact, you never did get no sleep. But we made it, by thick or thin, we made it.

Moreover, porters were required to use standard Pullman-issued blankets when they slept. Glenn goes on to recall, "The porter's blanket was blue. The Pullman blankets were brown, but the blanket for the porter's bed was blue. Now, if the inspector got on, and he didn't have that blue blanket, he suffered to have some days in the streets or maybe be fired, unless he could prove that there weren't any blue blankets on the car."[27]

Happy Davis, in his comments on those blue blankets, sees them as a conscious effort on the part of the Pullman Company to remind the porter of his inferior status and as a means to reinforce that status. He sees it as a symbolic social manipulation: it is not an instrumental job rule that is in operation here; rather, it is an extrinsic part of the occupational culture that is enforced by those in charge, which transcends tasks and duties. This fact of the porters' jobs, what it represents, and the ways the porters responded to it, enter us into the realm of folklife.

Happy Davis:

Never! The Pullman Company never forgot to let you know that you was *black*! The porter was relegated to sleep in the smoker. We had to sleep in the men's toilet. The Pullman Company, they let you know you was black, and you wasn't qualified to sleep under his best equipment. You could sleep under the sheets, but he had the blanket dyed blue, the mattress dyed blue. And if you were caught sleeping under anything other than that blue blanket, you'd be on the carpet. You couldn't take it, even if there wasn't but one blanket under the sofa in the men's room, and it was cold, you better *not* go out and get one of them brown blankets to put on that bed. The Pullman porter was relegated to sleep under that black blanket. If there was no smoking room, you had to take that black blanket with you and put it on your bed, because that's a constant reminder to you that you was black.

The porters' blankets were actually blue, but Happy refers to them as black. Noting the discrepancy, I asked whether it was a black blanket or a blue blanket. "It was a *blue* blanket," Happy answered. "They couldn't dye it black, because if they could have dyed it black they would have dyed it black. But it was blue."[28] The discrepancy is understandable since Happy is saying that the blue blankets were used to symbolize the second-class status of the black worker. The identification between blue blanket and black man in this case is for him so complete that he actually conjoins the two and begins to speak of black blankets.

Color symbolism was of great significance to porters. For instance, they were viewed by friends and family, and viewed themselves, as the *cream* of the crop, those Negroes special enough to qualify for the job of Pullman porter. Although some porters maintain that the company hired "the blackest men with the whitest teeth (a reference to the need to smile for the passengers), the company tended to hire lighter-skinned black men.[29]

Another small point, but an interesting one, occurs when Happy, apparently referring to the Pullman Company, says "he had the blankets dyed blue" rather than *they* or *it* had the blankets dyed blue. Who is Happy referring to, however inadvertently, when he personifies the Pullman Company as "he?" The conductor? George Pullman himself? Porters often seem to regard the Pullman Company as the living embodiment of its founder, and Pullman conductors as agents of his will, representatives of his almost mystic presence. As blue blanket and black man become a merged concept,

so do George Pullman, the Pullman Company, the Pullman conductors, and also inspectors and especially spotters become inter-
changeable.

Mr. L. C. Richie says of his early days:

> My experience on the Pullman car goes back a long, long
> time. My first experience with the Pullman Company, they
> did not have any place for the porter to sleep. And we
> couldn't go to sleep. That's in '26, 1926. Well, from 1926
> until '30, they didn't provide any place for a porter to sleep
> during those years. And they had inspectors on the train
> that would do nothing but walk through the train to see if
> the porter was asleep. And if he caught him asleep, they
> would bring him up, reprimand him for it, or give him time,
> or time off, or anything like that. You had to stay awake all
> night—you were supposed to. Now, you could, you know, sit
> in the corner, and they'd walk up and see you asleep, or
> something like that, and accuse you of being asleep. And
> you didn't have any union during those days, so naturally
> . . . any kind of punishment that they wanted to give you,
> they'd give you during those days. Those were rough days,
> before the union.[30]

The porter learned that the job he had so eagerly sought included many such hardships and inequities. For one thing, he had
to pay for his own uniforms, his own food, even the polish and rags
he used to shine passengers' shoes. More important were the three
occupational rules known to all porters: running in charge, doubling out, and P.M. time. The Pullman Company used these rules
to institutionalize discrimination in the days before the union.
Briefly, running in charge meant that the porter could be assigned
the duties of a conductor, in addition to his own work, but would
receive only $12 a month extra for it. The salary of a conductor in
1920 was $120 a month, while a porter's salary was $60, so the
company was able to save considerable amounts of money by cheat-
ing the porters. Doubling out meant that a porter could be ordered
out on a run immediately after having completed one, with no time
to rest or clean up, at a lower rate of pay. Finally, P.M. time was a
company time classification whereby a porter without a regular
run (known as an "extra" porter) would not be paid for any work
he did between the hours of noon and midnight. Even though a

porter had to prepare berths, stock linen, clean cars, and meet passengers prior to a run, if this work was done in preparation for a trip departing at midnight, it was done on P.M. time, and therefore, was not remunerated.

As might be expected, such blatantly arbitrary rules were of intense concern to porters and are the subjects of a great many narratives. C. L. Dellums, for instance, explains the P.M. time rule as he saw it and goes on to tell one of his experiences with the practice known as running in charge:

> They had other gimmicks. They had what you call P.M. time. The P.M. time didn't bother this guy that was on a regular run and didn't miss any time. But they had a small army of extra porters that had to stand by and be available to fill in for a regular porter who got sick or laid off for any reason. He's got to be sick to lay off, because he didn't make enough money to take a vacation. And then they'd use an extra porter.
>
> If they assigned an extra porter to go to work at any time after twelve noon, then he was going to work P.M., so he didn't go on the payroll till midnight. So then he would start out the next day 12:01 A.M., and that's when his pay would start. That was P.M. time, and they didn't pay.
>
> So, it was almost impossible for an extra porter to ever make sixty dollars, because most of the trains would leave P.M., particularly out here [in Oakland, California]. The porters would go in the yards, maybe five or six in the afternoon, make down the car with twenty-seven berths in it and make that car ready for the reception of passengers. And then they would open up at the station at nine o'clock. The porters would have to get out, assist the passengers and the baggage to get on board, and let them to bed if they wanted to. In some instances that train didn't move until after midnight.
>
> They had a few porters they called "in-charge" porters (those that could figure and keep records), because he had to do everything the Pullman conductor did plus the porter's job, taking care of that car and those passengers. All he got was $12.00 a month extra for running in charge. Before the Pullman Company went out of business, we had been able to bring the in-charge pay up to $32.50, I think it was. That still was a mere pittance for the work he was doing.
>
> One of the last trips I made was up to the Yosemite Valley, and while we were up there, they got in touch with

me through the ticket agent. There were going to be twelve cars coming out of there that night back to Oakland, and they didn't have any conductor to get up there to do it. So they told me, "Dellums, you take charge of those cars and bring them in." So, after I'd finished my work and made down those beds for my passengers, I had to go to all those cars that had porters on them and write up everything in that car that a conductor would have written up. So, then I get into Oakland the next morning, and I've gotta turn all this stuff in—the diagrams, all good. In my youth I was a damn good math'matician, always good with figures, so this stuff was spotless. They couldn't find a single error or mistake.

I got nothing for doing this. They paid me nothing; I was getting the extra twelve for running in charge. They knew I had the ability, so they made me in charge, but you can imagine how I felt.[31]

The experience was for Mr. Dellums a personal slight. The company is perceived as not only exploitative, but also actually mean-spirited and personally offensive. These job rules were seen as much more than economic injustices. Like the blue blanket, they were felt to be intentionally aimed at humiliating and perhaps even emasculating the porters.

In addition, status differentiations among porters were present; for example, an extra porter was lower on the ladder than the porter who was regularly assigned the car of the president of the United States. Also, certain runs were felt, at least by some porters, to be more prestigious than others because of the status level of the clientele they attracted, and, certainly, some runs were more lucrative. But the real status problems arose between the Pullman conductors and the porters generally. Not only did the conductors represent the company, but what was worse, they had no special skills that the porter lacked. The porter knew that he could do the conductor's job easily, and in fact he often did, under the in-charge proviso. But he was paid half of what the conductor made, and he was never given the opportunity to become a conductor himself.

Mr. L. C. Richie remembers that conductors were paid for entire trips, even though porters ran in charge for a portion of them.

Now, our conductor, when he'd get off to New York, or wherever he was going, he'd get the whole pay all the way through. But they would cut you down to two or three hours. You had done the work because you had picked up all the tickets, you've entered all the diagrams, and all he does is come back and pick up the tickets, the diagram, and everything, the call cards, and take the money, and he's got everything, and you sign for it. That's what they did.[32]

Porters remember the job as a series of indignities. They also remember much of their lives on the railroad fondly, but they do not separate out the indignities. Their occupational memories are a part of their lives today; these memories, whether totally accurate or shaped by time and later events, are the stuff of contemporary Pullman porter culture. Although the men are now old, those who are still alive are vibrant and vital: it is not a misnomer to refer to Pullman porter culture as contemporary, though one day soon it will be gone. These men went on to establish the first successful black labor union in U.S. history. They were active in the civil rights movement. Their experiences of deep-rooted, widespread racism and the humiliations they had to endure form a backdrop to those other activities. This is a kind of folk history: not only is it "what happened," it is what many men choose to remember and the way they understand what happened to them. Mr. E. D. Nixon of Montgomery, Alabama, describes the job in these words:

> Not only was it tough with the Pullman Company's demands upon you, but the hours was long, see. It weren't nothing for a Pullman porter to make three hundred to four hundred hours a month. To be able to do what the Pullman Company wanted him to do he had to make at least eleven thousand miles a month or equivalent to the hours it takes to make those eleven thousand miles. And then if you went over that and made an extra one thousand miles, they give you a dollar for it. Pat you on the back and say you done well and give you an extra dollar for a thousand miles.[33]

One porter tells a story of how he was once running in charge, and when it came time to collect the tickets, a passenger refused, saying, "I ain't never seen a nigger conductor before." L. C. Richie tells of an almost identical incident:

> These are days back when prejudices existed. And it was known all over at that time and recognized in those days. And I was a porter in charge. And that was in the thirties. . . . I was in charge, as I said before, and I was supposed to pick up the tickets, and all of that. Now this lady, she was a southerner. She didn't want me to pick up her ticket. Her reason was because I was black. She'd never

had a Negro to pick up *her* ticket, and of course, the white conductor that went along with me, he asked me why I didn't get her ticket. And I told him that she wouldn't give it to me. He said, "Why?" I said, "She never had a Negro to pick up her ticket." So he said, "If you don't . . ."—he went to her and said, "Now you give him your ticket." That was between Detroit and Buffalo, New York. We had to go through Canada—Windsor. (As you get out of Detroit, you go right under the tunnel and go into Windsor, Ontario.) He said, "You will give him your ticket, or else you'll get off at Windsor, the next stop." So she finally submitted and gave me the ticket.[34]

One can see from Richie's story that the porters were in an especially ambiguous position vis-à-vis conductors. Their work roles were in turn complementary and competitive. Added to this was the requirement that porters have their authority validated and their work substantiated by a white conductor, who claimed an authority that transcended occupational status because of his white skin. It is the racism of society in general that is framed in these stories, and the effects of that racism on how the porter's job was carried out.

Equally objectionable was the practice of using incognito "spotters" to write up any infraction of the rules that the porter might make. This was felt to be especially intolerable and demeaning, because the accused porter was not entitled to a hearing on charges that had been made without his knowledge by someone he did not know and never saw. "A spotter would run his finger along the windowsill and write you up for dust," say many porters. Because the porter was presumed guilty and the spotter never had to face the porter to substantiate the charges, the possibilities for abuse were many.

Porters certainly felt that the conductors, given the opportunity to be anonymous, took it. "Nine times out of ten," says Happy Davis, "a Pullman conductor who didn't like you would *put the pencil* on you and say it was the spotter. It broke your heart when you knew it was a lie." This comment brings up the issue of the relationship of the black porters to the white conductors. We can see from this comment, and from the preceding anecdote about "no nigger conductors," that the occupational situation of the porters was very much a part of, and a result of, a deeply ingrained racism in society as a whole, and that relationships between subordinates (porters) and superordinates (conductors) were intensified and polarized by this racism, just as the relationship between flight attendants (still usually female) and male pilots is complicated by sex roles. For instance, porters tell a joke in which a passenger asks a porter for the time. After he is told, the passenger goes to the conductor and asks the time again. The porter, curious, asks the passenger why he asked the same question of both the porter and the conductor. "Because I wanted it in black and white," he answered.

Bigotry was, of course, a general social problem, but porters faced a particular manifestation of it which can be called regional racism. This was the phenomenon of being treated differently in the South than in the North, sometimes by the same persons. On the surface, this statement might not seem too surprising, but I am referring here specifically to incidents wherein the difference in treatment in the North and in the South is highly contrasted. For instance, porters talk of dreading to go "through the tunnel" that runs under the Potomac River from Washington, D.C., to Virginia. Often passengers' behavior changed abruptly, according to porters' testimony. A passenger might start calling porters "nigger" instead of "porter." Once, a passenger insisted that a Negro passenger be removed from the coach as soon as the train had entered the South, even though he had not complained previously. In another kind of regional racism, Mr. Glenn tells of a roll call in the South in which the Northern porters were referred to as "niggers":

> From time to time during the war, hauling soldiers, I had the pleasure of going down there—I think it was down in Memphis—and you had to go in and sign up your name. And the woman there that would sign you up, she would call the main office, and when she called . . . she said, "Mr. Jones" (I don't know who the man was, this might not be the right name), she said, "I got two porters here from Atlanta, Georgia; I got three porters here from Miami, Florida; I got four niggers here from Chicago." Ain't that right, fellas? Ended up Mr. Bryce or Mr. Leach went down and fired the woman. We didn't look at it as segregation against us; we looked at it as the ignorance of those people themselves. In fact, we walked with our heads held higher than we felt their head was.[35]

Leon Long describes another racist incident:

> I had one passenger, I remember. He had a section, an upper and a lower [berth]. His wife slept in the upper, he slept in the lower. When time come to wake him up next morning,

going to Miami, why he told me, "Don't be rushing my wife." I told him, "I wasn't rushing her, I was only waking you up." We had one or two words like that. I said something kind of rough to him, and he went and got the conductor. He came back to tell the conductor what I said. He said, "I didn't know niggers were supposed to talk to a white man like that."[36]

This particular narrative is interesting because in it the porter is not portrayed as entirely blameless, insofar as he "said something kind of rough" to the irate passenger. The passenger's complaint to the conductor exhibits his racism, but that racism is couched as an indignation that a black man would ignore his station in life and speak as an equal to a white man. This is what the porter in the story did: by speaking "kind of rough" he responded as a man rather than as a subservient worker of the lowest social status. This simple act of rebellion, framed and presented in the greater number of porters' narratives throughout this book, and the struggle they portray—to be a man while being a servant—is a central issue in the porters' worldview and in their folk history.

A. C. Speight adds:

You had a whole lot going on that you wouldn't like. I guess you may have, in some instances, seen it like I've seen it, but I've seen it! I mean I've had people tell me, "I'll throw you off this train, nigger!" I'd say, "Oh, no, no, no—you don't throw me off the train. We throw one another off." So he didn't bother me no more. We had a whole lot of people that would give you a hard way to go. . . .

Well, this was in the South, because I was leaving Houston, Texas. I just walked by the man. He said, "Hey, nigger!" I kept going. "Nigger, do you hear me?" So his wife said, "You shouldn't say that." "Well, he's a damn nigger, ain't he?". . .

Another time we was down in Knoxville, Tennessee, waiting to go to New York, because they had an accident. A man got killed and some people got killed, and there were others that were living, and an ambulance came to get them. So when he came down there—I'm giving it to you just like the book wrote it now, or like the man said it—he looked over there at the fellow, and the ambulance was coming around, and the stretcher was coming by, he look, and—"Oh, a damn nigger." I ain't never had no more use for Tennessee since that.[37]

Ernest Ford:

I was a sassy porter. It depended on where I was, you see. If
I was up North, I acted like a northerner. It was "yeah, no,"
see. When I go South, with the conductor, it was "yes sir, no
sir." You govern yourself according to the area you are in.
But the conductor was like a gestapo over the porter. The
Pullman conductor was *worse* than the gestapo. The Pullman
inspector. All of them—they rode the porter as if he were
just a tool on that car.[38]

Relationships between porters and conductors were obviously
not good, as these words indicate. Racism, both internal and external to the job, immeasurably complicated the occupational relationships of superordinate and subordinate, which already tended
toward antagonism simply because of their structural relationship.
During the 1920s and 1930s, conductors and passengers operated
out of a context of *de jure* segregation—separation of the races de-
creed by law—and a white insistence on the doctrine of racial superiority. The Pullman cars themselves were segregated for the
passengers, as Ernest Ford recalls:

On the Crescent Limited, the Sunset Limited, all of the
southern trains, Silver Meteor as well, the Seaboard
Coastline, they had a partition that would come down all the
way and almost blind these two tables. And these two tables
were for colored who were dining. There are usually forty-
eight seats for diners, but only eight seats for colored. I've
been in a dining car full of colored people waiting to get to
one of these eight seats. And the majority of the forty seats
of the dining car for whites was vacant.[39]

A. C. Speight:

We had a place with two tables, two tables it was.
Regardless of who had to eat, you only had two tables and a
curtain up there. So, we got food that way. But most of us,
we called it "dead-head" equipment. You used to sign these
cars to go out all over the country, dead-heading, sometimes
on a freight train. Everywhere you stopped you couldn't get
nothing to eat. Nowhere you could get nothing to eat. So if
you didn't go back to that dead-head equipment, like for a
can of pork and beans and a box of soda crackers or
something like that, then you'd just starve.[40]

In such circumstances, the Pullman Company maintained that it was doing the black man a favor merely by employing him; the concept of equal pay for equal work was simply out of the question. Practices such as P.M. time, doubling out, and running in charge were easily rationalized. Job protection and fair representation were denied the porter, and he was rendered invisible and anonymous by being referred to by the generic name "George." Although the etymology of this term is debated by scholars,[41] the porters believe that they were called George because they were George Pullman's "boys." Just as they saw the company as George Pullman personified, they felt that being called George meant that they belonged to him. The sting of this indignity is especially painful because the practice is seen as a continuation of one that was born during slavery times: that of naming a slave after his master. We have come full circle then, back inescapably to slavery. The porter found himself constricted by this circle, which surrounded him and grew ever tighter, as the first quarter of the twentieth century passed.

NOTES

1. Anonymous. On some occasions men asked either not to be identified by name or not to be associated with certain quotes.

2. Jervis Anderson, *A. Philip Randolph: A Biographical Portrait* (New York: Harcourt Brace and Jovanovich, 1973), 158.

3. Ibid.

4. Stanley Buder, *Pullman: An Experiment in Industrial Order and Community Planning, 1880–1930* (New York: Oxford University Press, 1974), 7–27.

5. Anderson, 158.

6. Ernest Ford, Jr., May 1, 1978.

7. William H. Harris, *Keeping the Faith* (Urbana: University of Illinois Press, 1977), 2.

8. Ernest Ford, Jr., July 2, 1978.

9. Leon Long, November 12, 1980.

10. C. L. Dellums, November 17, 1980.

11. See William Wiggins, " 'They Closed the Town Up, Man!': Reflections on the Civic and Political Dimensions of Juneteenth," in Victor Turner, ed., *Celebration: Studies in Festivity and Ritual* (Washington, D.C.: Smithsonian Institution Press, 1982), 284–95, on the issue of the actual dates of emancipation.

12. See Karmela Leibkind, "Dimensions of Identity in Multiple Group Allegiance: Reconstruction through Intergroup Identification," in Anita Jacobson-Widding, ed., *Identity: Personal and Sociocultural* (Uppsala: Almqvist and Wiksell International, 1983), 187–204.

13. A. C. Speight, July 1, 1982.

14. Hunter Johnson, July 12, 1983.

15. Rex Stewart, November 13, 1980.

16. Ernest Ford, Jr., June 6, 1982.

17. Leon Long, July 7, 1982.

18. C. L. Dellums, November 18, 1980.

19. Congressman Ronald Dellums, November 17, 1980.

20. See for example Lawrence W. Levine, *Black Culture and Black Consciousness: Afro-American Folk Thought From Slavery to Freedom* (New York: Oxford University Press, 1977), 226.

21. Leon Long, July 7, 1982.

22. Homer Glenn, August 18, 1980.

23. Ralph Linton, *The Study of Man* (New York: D. Appleton-Century Co., 1936), 113–14. See also Ward H. Goodenough, "Rethinking 'Status' and 'Role,' " in M. Banton, ed., *The Relevance of Models for Social Anthropology*, ASA Monographs 1 (London: Tavistock, 1965).

24. I'd like to thank Roger Abrahams for his insights and help on this point.

25. Leon Long, July 7, 1982.

26. Fred Fair, March 30, 1983.

27. Homer Glenn, August 18, 1980.

28. Lawrence W. Davis, June 27, 1984.

29. Mark Workman drew my attention to the color symbolism apparent in the porters' words.

30. L. C. Richie, April 7, 1980.

31. C. L. Dellums, November 13, 1980.

32. L. C. Richie, November 14, 1980.

33. E. D. Nixon, May 27, 1981.

34. L. C. Richie, June 27, 1984.

35. Homer Glenn, November 13, 1980.

36. Leon Long, July 7, 1982.

37. A. C. Speight, July 1, 1982.

38. Ernest Ford, Jr., May 26, 1982.

39. Ernest Ford, Jr., November 13, 1980.

40. A. C. Speight, July 1, 1982.

41. Bernard Mergen, "The Pullman Porter: From 'George' to Brotherhood," *The South Atlantic Quarterly* 75 (1974): 224n.

George Pullman. *Chicago Historical Society, IChi 13920*

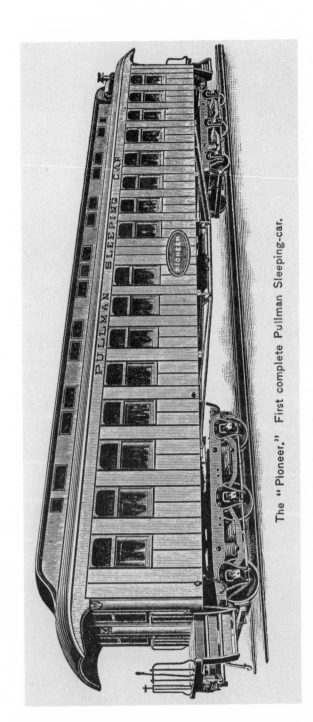

The "Pioneer." First complete Pullman Sleeping-car.

The Pioneer. Smithsonian Institution Photo No. 1372

Courtesy of the Colorado Historical Society

Photograph by Theo Marceau. *Courtesy of the Library of Congress*

Each passenger had personal service. *Courtesy of Santa Fe Railway*

A porter "breaks down" (prepares) an upper berth. Here he is attaching a curtain for privacy. Sleeping cars varied greatly, but many cars, such as this one, had twenty-two berths that the porter had to "make up" and "break down" daily. This had to be be done quickly and out of sight of the passengers. *Smithsonian Institution Photo No. 78-13870*

Mattresses for both upper and lower berths were stored in the upper one, with all other bedding. *Milwaukee Road photo*

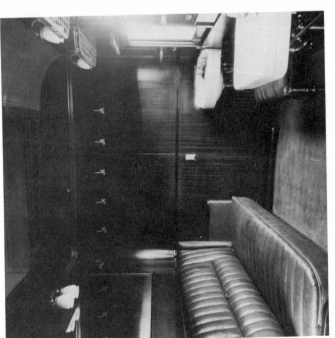

Pullman porters slept on the couch in the men's lounge, while all through the night people came in and out of the washroom. *Smithsonian Institution Photos Nos. P29516 and 77-7621*

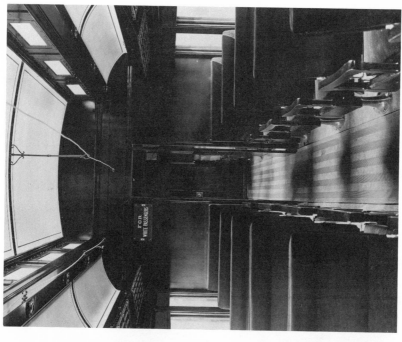

Segregation was a fact of life on the railroad. Smithsonian Institution Photos Nos. P13691 and P21315

On board the Pullman cars, porters mingled with wealthy white people that they would not otherwise meet. *South Florida Rail Sales*

Porters made passengers feel special by meeting them and taking their coats. *Courtesy of St. Louis-San Francisco RR*

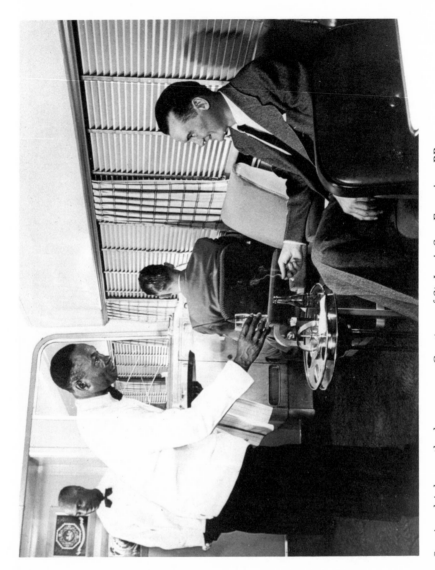

Serving drinks on the lounge car. *Courtesy of St. Louis-San Francisco RR*

2. Unionization

Central to any understanding of Pullman porters' culture is an appreciation of the role played by A. Philip Randolph in the formation of the Brotherhood of Sleeping Car Porters. The founding of the union and its eventual success are central events in the porters' sense of their history and their contributions as a group to society at large, even though between the years 1925, when the union was founded, and 1937, when it was recognized, the movement was joined by no more than half the working porters, at best.[1] Although a large number of porters, even a majority of them, objected to Randolph's activities at the time, porters today have incorporated the union movement into the construction of their personal identities. Men who were old enough to join the union in the 1920s and 1930s, but in some cases did not join until the 1950s, well after its success, nevertheless speak enthusiastically in favor of it. They did not join at the time, they explain, because they could not afford to risk their jobs, or even pay union dues. In fact, Randolph and his right-hand man, Milton P. Webster, had, on occasion, allowed porters to join the union without paying dues in an effort to swell the ranks.[2] In this chapter, we will look at those events—the establishment and empowerment of the union—through the eyes of the porters, and learn how they interpreted them and what they mean to the porters today.

For many porters, the world of 1925 consisted of widespread social injustice and occupational inequity and humiliation. In response, some men favored the formation of a labor union, while others were reluctant to do so openly, for fear of losing their jobs. Eventually, a group of Pullman porters in New York, led by Ashley L. Totten, approached a well-known labor activist named A. Philip Randolph for help.

In the past Pullman porters had attempted to form a union at least four times: in 1909, 1910, 1913, and in 1918, when an advocacy-oriented fraternal organization called the Brotherhood of Sleeping Car Porters Protective Union was initiated, only to be destroyed by the Pullman Company in 1920. Curiously, Pullman porters do not view these early attempts to organize as direct ancestors of the movement begun in 1925, possibly because these movements had failed. Nor do they perceive any direct historical continuity among them. In fact, the successful movement is often held up in contrast to these earlier movements. A. Philip Randolph is seen as tilting the balance toward success.

C. L. Dellums recounts:

> As we understand, there had been five previous attempts to organize Pullman porters. One we know about—the one prior to the Brotherhood. During the war . . . the President appointed a man from Atlanta, Georgia, by the name of William Gibbs McAdoo, to be the head of [the Department of Transportation]. McAdoo, to keep down strikes and trouble during the war, advised all the railroad workers to get together and form their unions—there was a number of them already formed, like the engineers and the Big Four group—and "send your representatives to Washington so that I can negotiate agreements with the government with you, in order to maintain peace and harmony in the railroad industry during this crisis." The transportation brothers had no trouble: they had unions, they just went down and got agreements. But when they got down to the smaller people, when they got down to the sleeping car porters and dining car people, there was nobody there to represent [them]. There were *five* different groups went down there claiming they represented the Pullman porters. Well, as we got the story years later, at least *three* of those guys were on Pullman payroll and sent by the Pullman Company. They didn't know each *other*, but each one was instructed not to agree with anything the other four brought forward: "Here's your program. And if they want a united organization, they all got to follow you." Well, if you have three people who are all taking the same position, obviously there's going to be no agreement, and therefore it collapsed.
>
> Now, in one of our conferences with Pullman officials several years after we had won the struggle, we asked them about this. One of the guys said, "Well, there were a few attempts to organize the porters before you guys came along." We said, "What happened to them?" They said, "We have them in the vault." We understood what they meant when they said they had them in the vault: they had the receipts in the vault; they were indicating that they bought

them up, they bought them off. So somebody said, "Well, what happened that those five attempts failed and your guys succeeded?" My first answer was, "They never had A. Philip Randolph."[3]

A controversial figure in American life, condemned by many as a communist, A. Philip Randolph is revered by retired Pullman porters as a genuinely great man of almost saintly integrity. Randolph embodied traits of honesty and intelligence that most Pullman porters felt were possessed by the rank-and-file workers. Randolph was not only admired, but also seen as an ideal, a representation of all the best characteristics of Pullman porters.

Asa Philip Randolph was born the son of a preacher in Florida in 1889, and his family moved to New York in 1911.[4] Always a precocious student, he attended New York City College and studied public speaking, history, political science, and philosophy. Maintaining that "the problem of people fighting each other was based on the fact that they were fighting a competitive system. Hence, the end result was conflict with each other," Randolph espoused socialism.[5] Working on behalf of his race, he recognized that gains in the economic sphere must accompany gains in civil rights. He also recognized that laborers, both white and black, were being pitted against each other.

Randolph felt that racism was used as a means of exploiting all workers. Abused white employees saw themselves as better off than their black coworkers, and they perceived black workers as threats to their jobs rather than as men in a similar situation. Randolph once said, "They had the stereotypes and myths of race and people, and looked at the myths and stereotypes instead of looking at the human being or the economic situation."[6] Later he would say, "My philosophy was the result of our concept of effective liberation of the working people. We never separated the liberation of the white working man from the liberation of the black working man. . . . The unity of these forces would bring about the power rally to achieve basic social change."[7]

By the 1920s, Randolph was famous as an orator and a labor organizer. Because of an attempt he made to organize porters in 1917, he had been fired from the railroad. He then organized a group of elevator operators and published a magazine called *The Hotel and Restaurant Messenger*. Later, the affiliation with the hotel was dropped, and the magazine became known as simply *The Messenger*.[8] Randolph would later use *The Messenger* as his primary vehicle for disseminating his radical philosophy concerning the establishment of a labor union of, by, and for blacks.

On September 15, 1921, the Pullman Company signed an agreement with Unit No. 122 of the Railway Employees Department of the American Federation of Labor. Although this was the first time the Pullman Company had ever signed an agreement with a labor union, it preceded the organization of the Brotherhood of Sleeping Car Porters by five years and established a precedent: that under the right circumstances, even an industrial giant such as the Pullman Company could be brought to the bargaining table. Eventually the company would enter into agreements with conductors' unions and shop employee unions. Its continued refusal to recognize the black porters' union under these circumstances was apparently motivated entirely by racism. White labor unions were recognized; a black union was not. Despite this, the white unions were closed to black workers: the so-called "Big Four" of the railroad unions (the Brotherhoods of Locomotive Engineers, Locomotive Firemen, Railway Trainmen, and the Order of Railway Conductors) all had specific rules banning black membership.[9] So the only recourse for black workers was to form a separate union, which the porters would attempt.

At around the same time, and in response to the porters' 1918 attempt to organize, the Pullman Company established its Employee Representation Plan. Presented as an alternative to a labor union, which was said to be communistic, the ERP channeled antimanagement grievances and was an attempt by the company to shatter the 1918 Brotherhood of Sleeping Car Porters Protective Union, as well as any future efforts to organize.

Porter Ashley L. Totten of New York was elected as a delegate to a wage conference in 1924. A small wage increase of $7.50 a month was granted, but Totten and some others realized that the ERP was ultimately a tool of the company, used to maintain the status quo among its porter workers. This realization, along with the continued existence of unfair labor conditions, led to the formation of the Brotherhood of Sleeping Car Porters in 1925. A group of porters, led by Totten, recognized in Randolph precisely the qualities of leadership they knew were necessary if the difficult attempt to organize Pullman porters (and the almost insurmountable task of defying the Pullman Company) were to be successful. Randolph also offered a proven and demonstrated dedication to the principles of labor organization, and because he himself was not a porter, he could not be co-opted or coerced by the company with threats of being fired or of punitively being assigned unattractive runs.

For his part, Randolph saw the porters as an ideal group to carry the message of black unionism throughout the country: because the porter worked on the railroad, his home was "everywhere."[10] He accepted Totten's offer to lead the new union, and in 1925, in an Elks Lodge in Harlem, The Brotherhood of Sleeping Car Porters was born. "Fight Or Be Slaves" was the motto the Brotherhood adopted. W. H. Des Verney, a porter who had thirty-seven years of job experience, was made vice president; porter Roy Lancaster was made secretary-treasurer, and A. Philip Randolph became president. As president, he would work closely with, and rely upon, the officials of the local chapters, and especially with the area vice presidents of the International: Milton P. Webster in Chicago, Ashley L. Totten in New York, Benjamin Smith in Detroit and Pittsburgh, E. J. Bradley in St. Louis, and Morris "Dad" Moore in Oakland, who was joined in 1928 by C. L. Dellums.[11]

All of these men had been porters before working for the union. "Dad" Moore was an elderly, caustic, cantankerous, and pensioned porter on the West Coast. When he assumed the job with the Brotherhood as organizer, he risked losing the small pension he was receiving. Risk it he did, and because of this, and because of his colorful personality, Dad Moore became one of the Brotherhood's early heroes. C. L. Dellums, who worked closely with him, assumed the position of secretary-treasurer for the Oakland division in February 1928, and today he speaks fondly of his former mentor:

He was a two-fisted, vulgar old man who was quite a scrapper. He and I became very close friends. Dad and I worked together, and we took advantage of his situation, his age, and his militancy. We talked about "the spirit of Dad Moore"—and it spread clear across the nation. It was used by the local divisions to help their unions.[12]

Operating out of the Oakland base, Dellums had a brief career as a porter before he was fired for his union activities. In fact, he was one of the founding officers of the Brotherhood of Sleeping Car Porters. He remembers his early involvement with the union:

In 1925 we heard about some man in the East writing about organizing the Pullman porters into a union. And of course I had been there just long enough to see what the conditions were, and I had sense enough to know that this guy was on the right track (whoever he was), talking about organizing the porters into a union. And his name was A. Philip Randolph. . . .

As soon as APR started issuing some literature, the porters running to Oakland from Chicago brought some out for us. That's how we *got* literature *from* [the union], and when we saw the address, we then could write to New York and get on the mailing list and get literature. We got application blanks and started organizing. And we developed quite an organization in Oakland. We built a good union there.[13]

Other porters who would become active in union activities remember their first exposure to union philosophy, and to Randolph himself. Mr. E. D. Nixon, of Montgomery, Alabama, recounts hearing his first union speech, and the subsequent threat to his job. Mr. Nixon handled the attempted intimidation quite skillfully:

In 1927 I was running to St. Louis, Missouri, and a man from Nashville came in my car, who was a porter also, in the early morning and told me, he said, "You know, Randolph, who is trying to organize the porters, is going to speak in St. Louis today at the Pine Street YMCA." He said, "I'm going up to hear him. I wish you'd go along with me." I said, "Maybe I will go along with you." And when I heard him talk, he convinced me that he knew what he was doing. Although I didn't agree with some of the things he said. For an instance, at that time we were making seventy-two dollars and fifty cents a month. And he said that "if you stick with me, the day will soon come when I'll have you making a hundred and fifty dollars a month." I couldn't believe that, but I went along and put a dollar in the collection plate.

So when I got home, before I got off the train, the superintendent there told me, "I understand you attended the meeting of the Brotherhood yesterday in St. Louis." I said, "Yes I did." So he says, "I'll tell you right now, we're not going to have any of our porters attending the Brotherhood meeting." I says, "Well, if somebody told you I attended the meeting there, maybe they told you also that I joined yesterday." And before he could answer me, I said, "Of course, before I joined I thought about what lawyer I wanted to handle my case if you started to mess with my job. And that's what I'm going to do—I'm going to drag anybody into court that messes with my job." And I didn't even know a lawyer's name at that time. But I bluffed him out so that he didn't bother me. And from then on I was a strong supporter of A. Philip Randolph.[14]

Although porters tell a great many stories of personal experiences such as these, wherein the porter, threatened by the company or some other outside force, confronts the situation and is victorious, not all the men were so fortunate. The company did everything in its considerable power and with its considerable resources to crush the union. Pro-union workers were taken off regular assignments. Some were beaten. Some, like C. L. Dellums, were fired:

> I started work for the Pullman Company in January of 1924, and I got fired as a result of my union activities around the first of October of 1927.... Well, when I went over to see the superintendent, Mr. O. W. Snotty, he spent all of the time—he sat there for at least an hour—talking to me about my union activities. And he said, "All we're doing is furnishing you transportation over this country to spread this Randolph Bolshevik propaganda, you know. And Randolph gets his money from Mos-*cow* [rhymes with how]." I said, "Don't you know how to pronounce that word? That's not pronounced Mos-*cow*, it's pronounced Mos-*coe* [rhymes with doe]." I began to kind of rib him some. I saw my discharge on his desk when I went in, so I knew that I'm there to be discharged. So I just spent all of that time, and then he handed me my discharge, and I started to get up.
>
> He said, "Now Dellums, I want you to remember one thing. You're not being fired for your union activities. You're being fired for unsatisfactory service." Well, this was the first time in the conference he mentioned unsatisfactory service. I said, "In what way? I'm rated as one of your superior porters. Now what do you mean by unsatisfactory service?" And he said—well, he went through a whole lot of stuff. He said, "When you are in the train and it backs into the Oakland Pier, the word flashes all over the pier, train to train, car to car. The grapevine goes round: Dellums is on the platform, and Dellums is on such and such a car, and such and such a train. So the men were slipping away one by one, getting over there to see you. Because if there was any new propaganda, you had it. If there were any developments, you knew them, and you were there to tell the men. So they'd come to you. You didn't have to go to them; they'd come to you." I think that was the last trip, I believe it was the last trip.[15]

Dellums's memories are typical of those men who were in the thick of the struggle early on. He remembers situations of blatant injustice, and in a way that is consistent with E. D. Nixon's narrative, Dellums responded to this injustice by confronting it through deepening his union work. Although he had no choice but to accept the reality of this particular situation, he would deal with the general problem for the rest of his life. He explains his strategy:

> My father taught me to be angry but not bitter. He said, "See, if you stay angry too long, you get bitter. Don't do that. Get it over with and forget it. Relax. Get something else on your mind, something you can laugh about. Your mind will get back to it later." So I never forgot that, and I tried to govern myself that way, and I don't believe that I'm bitter about anything. I think I'll raise hell as long as I can try to adjust things, but I know how to fight and walk away. And if things aren't corrected, I'll be back to fight some more another day. You can bet on that.[16]

The Pullman Company mounted an offensive against the formation of the union on many fronts. While porters were being intimidated and punished, the company pushed its Employee Representation Plan as a way to co-opt the union and still appear to be a pro-labor, compassionate, fair business. This was a company-run "union" that was used to alert the Pullman Company to the presence and identities of those porters who were potential troublemakers, in the view of the company, because they came forth with grievances.

Not every porter was in favor of unionization, certainly. Many were against the idea, and others were afraid for their jobs or otherwise intimidated, or merely fearful of the repercussions of open support. The testimony of the porters regarding unionization is illuminating insofar as it sheds light on the way the union's organizing activities were perceived by at least some of the men at the time. Moreover, their individual opinions and attitudes have been corroborated as generally true, that is, as having been experienced by a great many other men as well.[17] Porter Fred Fair, who served President Roosevelt's car, has this to say:

> We didn't have a union, we had a company association. We had nothing, we didn't have anything. The company would do anything it wants, put you off your run for nothing, without any hearing or any consideration at all. They could just tell you to go home for five days or ten

days, and there wasn't anything you could do. Of course, after we got a union, you really couldn't fire me without a hearing.

When he [Randolph] first started, there wasn't much organizing you could do, above the boards. You had to sneak around homes and everywhere else and organize. We had men fired. Some of them got back, some of them didn't after the agreement was signed. Everybody didn't go [along with the union], because they were afraid of losing the job they *had*, you know, because so many of them *had* lost their jobs around the country.[18]

Porter William Harrington states the problem simply and directly: "They had a *company* union. Now, the company had their union there, and a lot of them voted for the company union, and you ain't never going to get nothing from a company union."[19] In 1883 porters made $12.00 a month; by 1915 they received $27.50; and in 1924 the monthly minimum was raised from $60.00 to $67.00 a month. The company always claimed that these figures were deceiving, because the porter's salary was augmented by tips. In this way, the company exploited the service nature of the job by using the tipping system as an excuse to maintain wages that were roughly half what the conductors were paid. At the same time, this system forced porters to hustle for tips, thus validating the stereotype it had created and perpetuated of the obsequious and subordinate, but crafty and scheming black servant. The tipping system was one of Randolph's early targets, something that he pointed to when making his demands for a fair living wage for Pullman porters.

C. L. Dellums remembers the early days of attempted unionization as a time of great difficulty and equally great resolve. We can see in his following narrative the beginnings of an emerging epic of struggle in the occupational culture of Pullman porters: the struggle to unionize, with A. Philip Randolph the hero at the center.

It was the darkest period of the union, and several of the union officials felt perhaps their noble effort had failed. They turned to Mr. Webster, myself, and Mr. Randolph and said, "It looks like this is the end. So we leave it up to you. If you want to fold up we understand, but if you can find any way out, let us know." And Mr. Randolph talked to Webster and myself and he said, "We can save the Brotherhood. We can find a way to win this fight. If we can keep the doors open in New York, Chicago, and Oakland, we'll survive. Now, let us join hands and pledge ourselves that we are going to save the Brotherhood, we are going to win this fight or we'll report to our gods the reason why. Let's pledge ourselves that nothing honorable will be too much of a sacrifice for us to save the Brotherhood. Now let's join hands and pledge ourselves that." I said, "But now wait a minute, chief. I'm not satisfied with the wording of this pledge. You've got a bad word in there. I don't know whether I should take it or not." He said, "What's that?" I said, "You've got that 'honorable' in it," I said. "Because I'm going to keep the doors in Oakland open. I don't know whether everything I do will be honorable or not, but I'm going to keep the doors open in Oakland." And suffice to say, the doors never closed in those three cities.[20]

Success did not come easily, and it seemed as if it would not come at all. Randolph's ideas were considered so radical that he was often denounced by black clergymen and in the black press by individuals and establishments fearful of upsetting the white power structure. The company used a policy of favoritism to reward porters who would report on other porters who had attended meetings or otherwise engaged in union activities. Such men were called by the porters "snitchers," or worse, "Uncle Toms," in a usage of that term that is specific to this occupation. Porters did not see themselves as Uncle Toms, as the public oftentimes did, simply because they shined shoes and cleaned cuspidors. Rather, they reserved the term for those men who betrayed and undermined unionization and sacrificed the welfare of the group for personal gain.

For example, porters tell of individuals who would bribe the dispatcher, who assigned trips, by bringing him a magazine with a five-dollar bill inside. Homer Glenn tells one such story:

We used the term "Tom," we as porters, because we had so many porters sometime that would go into the office. I never did it. I was always a watchdog for the union. Here's a man over here that hadn't been to work in a week, and there's a man over here that came in this morning, and he'd walk in and throw a magazine in the window and say, "There's a good article on page 19." And the guy says, "Thanks for the magazine." Look at page 19, and it's got five dollars in it. That man tonight would go right back out on the job. And there's a man with a family, been there for a week, still hasn't got a job. Those are the people we call Uncle Toms, people who pay off for jobs.[21]

Randolph realized he was up against a very large and powerful organization which could intimidate, corrupt, and otherwise coerce large numbers of rank-and-file workers, and he understood that he needed an equally powerful ally. In 1928 he agreed to join with the American Federation of Labor. Porters criticized him for this, because the AFL had neither welcomed blacks into its membership, nor had it supported black causes. Meanwhile, the company's bribings, firings, beatings, and propagandizing continued, and the porters held their union meetings secretly so as not to jeopardize their jobs. Also, the Ladies' Auxiliary of the Brotherhood of Sleeping Car Porters was formed by the wives of the porters. They raised money by holding bake sales, flea markets, and so forth. Mrs. Rosina Tucker, who was over one hundred years old and living in Washington, D.C., when I first interviewed her, was international secretary-treasurer of the Ladies' Auxiliary and president of the local chapter. The wife of a porter, she held secret meetings in her house on Seventh Street, NE, in Washington, and disseminated literature for A. Philip Randolph. Mrs. Tucker recalls:

> I got involved—I could *not* be involved if my husband was not a porter. You see, this is an organization for the porters, and I became involved as a member of the auxiliary. But before we had an international auxiliary, we had little clubs—like councils, we called them. And in that way all over the country, these councils would help the men to raise money and so forth. And I organized the council here in this very house, very early in the movement, and I was made president.
>
> So, we worked along, my group. We did teas, we did little dances and so forth. And sent it to New York to help them. And other auxiliaries, I suppose, did the same. That's why I say that the *women* were the ones who were the backbone, in that they furnished the money and encouragement to the officials. Now, we had a meeting at a certain home once, and the company found out that we had this meeting. So they called the husband in, the porter in, and asked him about it. The porter was able to show by his time sheet that he was out of town. But his *wife* held the meeting!
>
> The Women's Auxiliary got started almost the same time as the Brotherhood. We had these small groups of women in every city. And now, the International Auxiliary started in 1938, and I was the secretary-treasurer of that. . . .

We would have meetings, and Mr. Randolph would come down from New York to hold meetings. He'd spend the night with Mr. Tucker and me. Of course, it was dangerous because it was possible that my husband would lose his job, if the people—we call them stool pigeons—if they knew. So that's why we had to be very, very careful about our meetings. Mr. Randolph has stayed in my very home, and so has Mr. Totten. But I'd have to close my shutters. All of the materials came from New York to me.

Now, I collected dues very secretly. I'd go to the men's homes. Sometimes they came to me or met me somewhere and gave it to me. But I collected dues. The communications were sent to me, and I would inform the men as best I could.[22]

Mrs. Tucker tells a story about her actions when her husband was reassigned to a less desirable run because of her union activities. The story is another example of one type of narrative common so far: that which tells of active confrontation and demanding your rights. She tells us:

For instance, Porter Tucker came home one day and said that he'd been taken off his line. But my husband had a regular run, of course. When they had a new run put on, he was among the first to be given this run. They had to have at least five years experience and a record that was perfect to get on this run—I can't call the name of it now, but Broadway ... Broadway Limited, that's it—and he went out one day [to work] and came back. I asked him why he came back. He said they wouldn't let him go out. Said, "It's because of my activities." He 'called the name of the man, the sign-out man. They sent him out, but not on his run, the next day.

Well, I thought about it. And, oh, those days I was tough. I thought to myself, Now they're involving me. I am just not going to take it. They had no jurisdiction over me whatsoever. So, I called the Pullman office and asked to see the superintendent. . . . And I knew it was he on the phone. And when I said, "This is Mrs. B. J. Tucker," this man left the phone. Now, of course, everybody knew me. All of the porters knew me. And they converged and talked, you know. And some of them would talk to the white people. The officials and so forth, they knew me. And to think the superintendent wouldn't even talk to me.

Well, I was so upset that—I don't mean scared—but I went to bed, and the next morning I said, "I know what I'll do, I'll go over there." So, I went to the superintendent's office and told them who I was. Said, "He's in conference." I went into the station, wrote a note, sent it up by the . . . the Red Caps. And I wrote a note saying that it's very important. And he sent me word that he's in conference. And I knew then that he just didn't want to talk to me. I came back home, and called one of the Brotherhood men and told him what had happened. He said, "Remember, Mrs. Tucker, all you have to do is go to the official over him." He gave me his name.

So I went to the station and went into this office. As a rule there's a girl at the door, but the girl wasn't at the door. But I saw a man walking. I said, are you Mr. So-and-so? and he said, "Yes, I am." And as he talked, he walked to his office, and I followed him. And I told him, "I am Mrs. B. J. Tucker, and I want to know why my husband was taken off his run." He said, "Why are *you* taking it up? Why doesn't *Tucker* take it up?" I said, "The sign-out man said that *nothing in Hell* could move Tucker from that line but his wife's activities in the Brotherhood of Sleeping Car Porters." I said, "You put my husband back on his line, or *I'll be back!*" Well, it was amusing because he seemed to have a fear, because a black woman would come to a superintendent, with the power he had, and speak to him in that manner. Well, the next time, my husband got back on his run.

Now there had been other times that porters had been penalized for certain things. Their wives would go and *beg* for them, *plead* for them, "*Please* take my husband back." But Sister Tucker didn't do that![23]

Mrs. Tucker tells quite a story. The words emphasized in the text are attempts to duplicate the stresses in her original utterances. Like the narratives of C. L. Dellums, her stories praise self-determination and resistance in the face of overwhelming odds. They present A. Philip Randolph, and the movement he led, in the highest of terms, and along with that, a tiny bit of self-aggrandizement may have crept in. She presents herself as important, as does Dellums, because of her early and close connection, and unswervering dedication, to Randolph and the integrity of the cause.

This attitude of defiance, from Randolph on down, saw the Brotherhood through to eventual victory. Once, in 1928, Randolph threatened a strike action against the company, but did not actually call for one. At the time, this was seen by many, including some porters, as a retreat from his militant posture, but it is now generally conceded that Randolph was correct in his choice. The fact was that chances were too great that the porters would lose everything. During this time period, the BSCP had petitioned the Interstate Commerce Commision to investigate the legality of tipping. Arguing that the practice compromised the quality of service, and that the Pullman Company was in effect a public utility, Randolph hoped to end tipping and so force the Pullman Company to raise wages. The ploy was a controversial one, and it cost Randolph the good will of thousands of porters. Eventually, the ICC ruled that the issue was not in its jurisdiction to decide, but in the meantime, the gains the union had made among rank-and-file workers were threatened. Porters depended on tips, and did not want to see their primary source of income done away with.[24]

In 1934, however, President Franklin Delano Roosevelt signed into law legislation that in effect banned company unions, under the National Industrial Recovery Act and the Emergency Railroad Transportation Act. This legislation encouraged employers to arrange for fair working conditions with employees. Certain guarantees were made to labor; one of these explicitly granted workers the right to organize and elect leaders of their own choosing with no adverse interference, influence, or restraint from management. This legal guarantee was interpreted by the courts as outlawing company unions such as the Pullman Employee Representation Plan. The passage of this legislation was, of course, a great boon to the struggling BSCP.

Mr. William Harrington of Washington, D.C., sees it as the turning point for the Brotherhood. What is interesting about his testimony, and the other testimony thus far, is the way in which history is personalized and framed within the contours of the occupational group. Each individual has his or her own experiences, each has seen certain things, heard certain stories. Each builds his or her own presentation of self out of these experiences; thus we have Mr. Dellums and Mrs. Tucker telling stories of their own heroism along with that of Randolph, Webster, and Totten. The testimonies are also shaped by group concerns, however, and are important as being representative of group aesthetics as well, both in terms of the occupation (the proper way to behave as a Pullman porter) and narrative aesthetics (what properly constitutes a story and the proper way to tell it). The testimony and the narratives enrich the documentation we have of historical events by giving us a window into both the individual and group dynamics that shaped them, and in turn, a picture of the men and women who were shaped by them. Mr. Harrington says:

> Before 1936, your superintendent would put a yes-man on a run and nobody could bump him. Your seniority was nothing. And that's the way it was up until 1936. We got the first agreement with the Pullman Company. Of course, we didn't get that until Franklin D. Roosevelt. When he first came in, he passed a law that we could form a union without interference from your employer. And that's when you could legally join a union without being fired or being laid off. Of course, the union was formed before that time, but you had to *slip* to meetings, and it was something like an underground movement, see? Because when the Pullman Company found out you attended a union meeting, you were probably laid off. He tell you to go home until he sent for you. And you may be home a week, or two weeks, but they would punish you, hearing that you attended union meetings.
>
> When that law was passed, it knocked all the stool pigeons out, what we call stool pigeons, that run to the superintendent, carrying news to the superintendent. Some men would cut your throat to make good with the superintendent. In 1927, we were afraid to join. I didn't join until 1929.[25]

The patience and endurance of these long-suffering men were rewarded. On August 25, 1937, twelve years to the day since the first Brotherhood meeting in Harlem, the Pullman Company surrendered. They signed the first agreement ever made between a large American corporation and a union of black workers. This was a historic moment: never before had a major industrial giant signed an agreement with a labor organization of black men; never before had black men successfully organized. Randolph realized that rather than play roles of submissiveness and subservience and rely upon the hoped-for beneficence of white people, rather than act out the routines and stereotypes that had been nurtured in their job roles, the porters must unionize, for their strength lay in organization. Blacks had previously been viewed as strikebreakers by white workers, because they were used as such by white industrial management. Now, however, they were leading the way, demonstrating that you must deal with injustice head on and demand your rights.

The irony that the agreement was signed on the twelfth an-niversary of the founding of the union did not go unnoticed, as recounted by C. L. Dellums:

> We were a handful of Negroes. Had nothing: no money, no experience in this. I used to say that all we had was what God gave the lizard.
> We succeeded after twelve long, bitter, expensive years. Somewhere between five hundred and one thousand men were discharged from the Pullman Company as a result of their union activities or their open support of the union. All the money we could rake and scrape was put in that struggle. But fate also played a trick, because the federal mediator was running the negotiations, and he got us together in 1937, and we signed the contract with the Pullman Company on August 25, 1937. When the mediator mentioned the fact that this was an historical occasion—the contract signed on the twelfth anniversary—the Pullman people got angry all over and accused us of maneuvering something for propaganda purposes. The mediator had to bawl them out and tell them it didn't have a damn thing to do with it: "I was running the show," he said. "You could have readjusted the day to the day before, but you people are the ones who gave in last and signed the agreement." Well, that was the first economic agreement that was ever signed in this country by Negroes with a white institution and virtually showed the Pullman Company where to sign. That was a tremendous thing. It was a great inspirational thing to the entire race.[26]

The signing of the agreement in 1937 meant immediate gains for the porter, including the largest single raise in pay they had ever received from the company. Minimum monthly pay jumped from $77.50 to $89.50, while the maximum went from $88.50 to $100.50. Previously, in 1926, monthly minimum wages had been increased from $67.50 to $72.50. At the time, the company main-tained that this 1926 raise was evidence of the efficacy of the Em-ployee Representation Plan, but Randolph and members of the union felt that it was in fact a reaction to the efforts of the porters to organize outside the company union. With the signing of the 1937 agreement and the concomitant jump in pay, Randolph appeared to have been correct.

This juxtapositioning of events, and the way that only certain events become fixed in the narratives of porters and framed as significant (e.g., illustrating the "darkest days" or honor in the face of adversity), are evidence that the narratives are a kind of folk history, or ethnohistory. The term "folk history" does not in any way suggest that the events described are false, but rather, that they are being presented as part of a view of the history of the Pullman porters as seen and understood, and made meaningful, by the participants in that history. A case in point is this story C. L. Dellums tells about a meeting with Champ Carry, the vice president and negotiation representative of the Pullman Company, after the success of the union. He tells it dramatically, then draws a moral from it—one that is central not only to the porters' perception of the character of A. Philip Randolph and the success of the union movement, but also to their images of themselves:

> So, maybe a couple of years after that [the signing of the agreement by Mr. Carry], we were down there for something, and the man who was the head of the Pullman Company was named Champ Carry. I guess his name was Champ—that's all we ever heard. And he said to Mr. Randolph, "Would it be an imposition for me to ask for a conference, Mr. Randolph, with you and Mr. Webster and Mr. Dellums? I just want to sit around and talk. We're friends now these days." I said, "You mean friendly enemies."
>
> "Well, we get along," he said, "nowadays, and let's talk. I think we're doing pretty good." And he said, "Now let's be frank about this thing. Here was a handful of colored people. Negroes. Got together here and took on the Pullman Company! You know the Pullman Company is one of the most powerful industrial institutions in the nation. How in the hell did you figure to win? We knew you were crazier than hell. There was no way to win. But you did! And we're still wondering, how in the hell did you do it?"
>
> So, Mr. Randolph said, "Well, Mr. Carry, we thought about it a lot, we talked about it a lot—we're not too certain ourselves how we won. But I guess we could summarize it by saying dedication, and integrity."
>
> We were fortunate that A. Philip Randolph came along. Randolph was the greatest orator that ever lived. He was nearest to a perfect orator that I ever saw on the platform. He was a brilliant man, a very able man. I could describe A. Philip Randolph in one word: integrity. A man of great stature and integrity. And that's what he was. And that's

what we developed in the Brotherhood.We succeeded because of the leadership of A. Philip Randolph. Randolph I would describe to young people today as the Martin Luther King of his day.[27]

In Dellums's skillful telling, he sets the president of the company as being somewhat solicitous of the now-victorious Randolph ("Would it be an imposition . . ."). Dellums also paints a picture of a group of struggling men who not only were at a distinct disadvantage vis-à-vis the Pullman Company, but were also at a profound social disadvantage, because they were a "handful of colored men" who began with nothing. Thus Dellums sets up and recapitulates the heroic struggle, with its David-and-Goliath qualities, through the words of the representative of the Pullman Company. This allows the victory to be savored ever so sweetly, as it posits a coming to David, a leveling of status and a recognition of equality, if not superiority, in the adversary. How did all this come about? Through the heroism of the black leader A. Philip Randolph, a heroism whose shape is defined in a single word of profound importance to porters: integrity.

William Harrington and E. D. Nixon both echo Mr. Dellums's sentiments. According to Harrington,

Randolph made a job out of it. Yes, indeed. And I'll always admire him and give him credit. He didn't sell us out. He's one out of a million that wouldn't, didn't sell us out.[28]

E. D. Nixon:

He said, "I'll get you $150 a month." Everybody thought he was a damn fool then, but he sure got it. And in later years, Mr. Randolph had a meeting with us. And Mr. Randolph stated to us there that we will have Negro firemen and Negro engineers [on the railroad]. And we told him, like this, "Chief, you're crazy. We don't believe it." He said, "In the next two months, you'll have a Negro engineer." And two months later, West Pine, Georgia, had a Negro engineer. He never talked out of two sides of his mouth. When he told you something, that's what it was.[29]

In the same year that the porters' salaries were raised, 1926, the Pullman Company established the policy of featuring a name card in each car so that passengers would no longer have an excuse to call porters "George." If a passenger did this, the porter could refer him to the name on the card. The Pullman Company informed porters that they need not respond to the name "George" and that no disciplinary action would be taken against them for refusing to respond. At a time when the BSCP was trying to discredit the ERP as a bad-faith organization, this tactic allowed the company to take credit for abolishing the use of the offensive sobriquet "George," although in fact, the generic use of the name continued for years. Randolph and the BSCP claimed that the company was in fact caving in to the demands of the BSCP and trying to save face by appearing to have initiated the move. At the same time, the company was attempting to undermine the union by addressing some of the grievances underlying its formation. To the present day, porters favor this interpretation: that it was the formation of the union that was the real cause of these advances. Not surprisingly, they place the credit for the name-card innovation with A. Philip Randolph.

William Harrington:

> They used to have a meeting every month, and they'd say "you boys," and Randolph stopped them from *that*. In the agreement. You call them *men*. After the agreement, they had to call you *men*.[30]

Lawrence W. Davis:

> The BSCP was the greatest organization known to mankind. We even had our name card to put up on the front of the car, with your name on it so the passengers wouldn't call you "George" or something. He had to refer to you by your name that was on your name card. All before then, a porter was liable to be any damn thing: "George," anything they want to call you. "Boy," anything else. Passengers called me everything but a child of God! But I laughed it off. I don't *get* insulted long as you got some money, you understand what I mean. Porters didn't like it though. You'd be surprised how proud the Pullman porter is. Pullman porter's a *proud* man.[31]

The changes and improvements did not come all at once, but over the years the union did away with the practices of doubling out, P.M. time, and running in charge. Years later, in the 1950s, Mr. Randolph himself commented on the union's successes in an address he made to the men and their wives in Chicago. Even more important than the economic breakthrough the union achieved was the dignity and self-respect the union afforded the porters. Interestingly, it is this aspect of the ramifications of the union that Mr. Randolph focuses on in the following testimony.

It can be truthfully stated that the Brotherhood has achieved job security. Before these agreements existed, porters were unceremoniously fired upon the slightest pretext. It was practically unknown for a porter, when once discharged, for anything, to be restored to his job, without the said porter crawling upon his belly, and with great humiliation, begging his boss for another chance.

What of wages? In this connection it is no exaggeration to say that before the Brotherhood championed the cause of the porter, this class of workers were not only the industrial paupers on the railroads of the United States and Canada, but pitiful beggars, with hands outstretched for the alms of gifts. Yes, the Brotherhood took the porter out of the lap of industrial and public charity, and made him a self-respecting worker. It brought, for the first time, sunshine, cheer, comfort, some luxury, and hope into the porter's home for his wife and children.[32]

Mrs. Tucker sees the activities of Randolph and the other union leaders as having had far-reaching consequences, not only on the porters at the time, but also on later generations of porters' families, and on black people in general throughout the United States.

The Brotherhood brought out qualities of strength and courage in the porters and their wives. They became leaders in their communities, bought homes, and sent their children to college. Thus the porters were able to give their sons and daughters the opportunities they themselves had been denied, to become lawyers and teachers and businessmen. As an organization, the Brotherhood laid the foundation for the civil rights movement in this country. It inspired black people by proving that they could organize and get results. For example, there was the Ladies' Auxiliary which raised money and supported the work of the Brotherhood during its darkest days. I, myself, was the international secretary-treasurer and president of the local here in Washington, D.C. In the labor movement, the American Federation of Labor had always resisted black membership until the Brotherhood broke down those barriers. The porter changed the image of blacks from strikebreakers to strong union men. And in 1941, Mr. Randolph forced President Roosevelt to create the Fair Employment Practices Commission by threatening a mass march on Washington by thousands of black people.

Years later, he organized the famous 1963 March on Washington.[33]

Mrs. Tucker speaks for porters generally when she says that Randolph forced Roosevelt to create the Commission. Again, he is perceived and described as heroic. Randolph continued to serve as president of the union after its recognition and continued to fight for improvements in labor conditions and for advances in civil rights in general. As such, he was seen by porters as a persevering warrior, one who won in the long run through persistence and sheer moral rectitude. In itself, the union's recognition was a blow struck for civil rights, because it changed the public image of Negro workers from supposed strikebreakers to committed unionists. In addition, Randolph and the Brotherhood contributed to the cause of civil rights in many direct ways. It was, in fact, a Pullman porter, Mr. E. D. Nixon of Montgomery, Alabama, who organized the famous bus boycott in that city in December, 1955, after the arrest of Mrs. Rosa Parks.

The relationship of the labor movement to the civil rights movement is evident here. Mrs. Parks had refused to give up her seat to a white man and move to the rear of the segregated bus. After she was arrested, she called her friend and former employer E. D. Nixon to throw her bail. Porter Nixon, besides being active in the BSCP, had been president of the local chapter of the National Association for the Advancement of Colored People (NAACP). During the events that led to the boycott of the Montgomery bus lines by the city's black people, Nixon helped to bring the young Reverend Martin Luther King, Jr., into the foreground of the civil rights movement. Mr. Nixon, and porters today, point to this fact with some pride as yet another case of the enormous contributions made to this country by the BSCP, porters, and A. Philip Randolph. The Brotherhood supported the Montgomery strike with much-needed funds, and Nixon's labor-organizing skills were put to good use.

E. D. Nixon says of that time:

> They arrested Mrs. Parks for refusing to obey the bus driver who was driving the bus when he asked her to get up and give her seat to a white man. She didn't get up, and they arrested her and threw her in jail like a common criminal. So I made bond for her, and I said to Mrs. Parks, I said, "You know what? I'd like to use your case to break down segregation on the buses." And I recorded a number of names on a tape recorder that night, and I started calling them and telling them about what happened. I said, "It's my

decision that we organize a bus boycott and fight discrimination on the buses." Ralph D. Abernathy, who most of you may have heard of, was the first man I called. He said, "Yeah, Brother Nixon, I'll go along with you." And I called the next man, Reverend H. H. Hubbard, and I expected him to go along with me because, number one, he was the president of the Minister's Alliance, and number two, he's my pastor at the church I went to, so I didn't expect him to fight me. The third person I called was Martin Luther King, and he said, "Brother Nixon, let me think about it awhile and call me back." So I went on and called eighteen other people. I called him back and he said, "Yeah, Brother Nixon, I decided I am going to go along with you." I said, "I'm glad you decided to go along with me, Reverend King. Your church is the only church right downtown, and I told eighteen other people to meet at your church this evening at three o'clock. It would look kind of bad to have that many people at your church for a meeting of this kind and you weren't there." He said, "Well, I'm going to be there." I said, "All right," so I set up this meeting.

And that was Friday, December 2, and Sunday morning, December 4, headlines were "Negroes Boycott the Montgomery City Line." And, of course, I got hold of the paper that morning, and it was a very good story. I called every minister in town and said, "Have you read the paper this morning? Read it. Take it to church with you and tell the people in church that we want to have 2,000 people there at the Holt Street Baptist Church tomorrow night." And instead of 2,000 people, the paper said we had 4,500. I know Montgomery about as well as any newspaperman, and if we didn't have 7,500 people we didn't have a soul. And if I hadn't known anything about organized labor, you wouldn't have had them out there. And then after that, that's when Reverend King came into the picture. He was elected that night.[34]

This view of the modern civil rights movement as having sprung from the work and expertise of a Pullman porter and member of the BSCP is shared not only by other porters, but by historians of the era. The particular importance of these events to porters and their self-image is evident in the emphases Mrs. Tucker used when she referred to them: "But I want it to be *known*, that the *humble Pullman porter*, the man who had been *kicked* around, and *shoved* around, and *worked* without adequate pay, was the man that *stimulated* and *worked for*, and *fought for*, this boycott in Montgomery."[35] Mrs. Tucker said this with great force, and she reinforced her emphases by slapping her hand on the arm of her chair as she spoke. Nixon himself makes the connection of his skills and his work to the Brotherhood quite explicit, when he says:

> I was able to make a contribution solely because we had the Brotherhood, and I wasn't afraid. And, again, I have to come back to A. Philip Randolph. In my judgement, A. Philip Randolph was the greatest black man we had in the last one hundred years. The civil rights movement saw to it that black people were able to do things legally, like ride on a Pullman car, say. But the labor movement saw to it that black people had the money to buy the ticket to ride on the Pullman cars, see? What good is it to have the right to do something, if you don't have the money to do it? The labor movement gave black people the opportunity to do things that the civil rights movement gave the right to do.[36]

Martin Luther King, Jr., figures prominently in what is perhaps A. Philip Randolph's greatest achievement in the field of civil rights: the 1963 March on Washington. Organized and led by Randolph, it was at this historic demonstration that King delivered his famous "I have a dream" speech. The martyred King is recognized nationally today as a great man, a man whose day of birth is commemorated by a national holiday in January. Randolph is less well known, less celebrated; but among porters he is generally considered the greatest black man of the twentieth century, a fearless and charismatic leader, a perfect and compelling orator, and a friend of the rank-and-file worker. As we shall see, the image that porters have of Randolph is essential to the image they have of themselves.

A. Philip Randolph died in New York on June 30, 1979, at the age of ninety. Ernest Ford, Jr., a Washington, D.C., porter, says that he was the Martin Luther King of his day, and that "he was to the black labor movement—he was to the black *man* in the labor movement—what the NAACP was to the black man in the legislative movement."[37] At first Mr. Ford began by describing Randolph's importance to the movement, an abstract thing. He quickly corrected himself and personalized the statement: Randolph was important to the individual *man* in the movement.

Porter Homer Glenn from New York says:

> At the March on Washington, you can go out today among the black people, and you can take a thousand dollars with

you and bet everyone you see a thousand dollars that
Randolph was the head of the March on Washington, and
they'll say King. Everyone will bet King. But Randolph was
the man who set up the March on Washington. Bayard
Rustin was the chief lieutenant. People got it in their mind
that King was the man.[38]

One cannot overstate the eminence with which Randolph is
regarded by the porters who knew him or heard him speak. Nor is
it possible to overestimate the value and importance of the union
to a generation of black men and their families. The Brotherhood
is credited by them as being the organization through which dis-
affected blacks gained control over their destinies, economically,
morally, and personally. Porter William D. Miller, the last president
of the Washington, D.C., local of the BSCP often reminisces that
he used to serve the president of Smith College on his car, and
now, he says proudly, "my daughter goes there."

The union allowed porters an economic opportunity that had
been denied to them, and they won it through years of struggle,
endurance, suffering, and unimpeachable honesty. Mr. Dellums
names it in his story about meeting with the Pullman officials:
integrity. He goes on to add:

> The Pullman Company could no longer take away a porter's
> job because it didn't like the color of his eyes or the way he
> parted his hair. They had to have a reason, and the reason
> had to stand up. We squeezed an agreement out of these
> people that no other union in the country reached. We had
> an agreement that the Pullman Company had to prove the
> man guilty beyond a reasonable doubt. No other union in
> the nation had such a clause as that. . . . Besides the
> increased pay we got, the improved working conditions,
> eventually a forty-hour week, I would say the next most
> significant thing the Brotherhood provided—not only a
> platform but provided—was an avenue through which its
> leaders could participate in the overall civil rights struggle,
> with a salary, and ample time to keep up their work.[39]

Mrs. Tucker says:

> This union lifted the status of the Pullman porter. And from
> their forty dollars that they started out, they began to make
> one hundred, two hundred, three hundred dollars a month—
> better working conditions. And those very people—because
> I've had some of these schoolteachers say to me, "Mrs.

Tucker, please get me a Pullman porter for a husband." So
you can see how ... the union made these porters feel that
they are somebody. I think of Jesse Jackson, "I am
somebody." And that's what this Pullman porter did. And it
also encouraged other groups of people.[40]

Leon Long:

Randolph raised up our standard of living. Every porter had
a different look on life; he felt that he had better treatment.
When they first started, they made arrangements that you
had to be off so many hours. You had to have sleep, even
during the daytime. They'd come back and say, "You're off."
You can go up into the coaches somewhere and sit down,
relax, and talk. You got so many hours, you got to get some
rest ... you had somewhere you picked where you could
sleep. You didn't have to sleep in the smoking room.[41]

William Harrington:

A. Philip Randolph—that's the man put us on our feet, that's
the man got me sitting right here in this house, paid for, and
nothing to worry about. If it wasn't for that [the union], the
Pullman Company, if you retired before that, you got a
dollar for every year you worked for the Pullman Company.
That's all you got, one dollar. If you worked forty years, you
got forty dollars. But Randolph, he labored out there, and he
caused it to come under the Railway Labor Act.[42]

Mrs. Tucker continues her explanation of the deep social ramifications of Randolph's life and leadership, and of the porters' union.
According to her (and the men quoted along with her), the union
had profound effects on the families of porters and paved the way
for a black middle class in this country. She says:

Not only were these men helped financially, they were
helped educationally. They grew in knowledge, and they
were able afterwards to do things that they never dreamed
of doing before. Now I know when we had these meetings,
they couldn't get up and talk. They were loyal, they'd keep
the rules and that, but some of them didn't even know how
to make a motion. And they learned that. They learned how
to stand up and boldly make a report. And then they became
interested in things of the city that they lived in, of the
country, and so forth. And there was a great improvement in
these men—and women. One man in Baltimore became a

member of the state assembly, and we had one in St. Louis who became a state senator. The Brotherhood encouraged men to go to school. We had one or two porters who became lawyers. And we had porters whose children became doctors and lawyers and so forth. It was a benefit in almost every area of life, for these men. It was wonderful.[43]

One man who is living proof of the far-reaching opportunites provided by the Brotherhood for later generations is Ronald Dellums, U.S. congressman from Berkeley, California, who is C. L. Dellums's nephew. Ronald's own father was a porter, briefly, and as we have seen, his uncle was seminal in the establishment of the history-making Brotherhood of Sleeping Car Porters. When he discusses the servile nature of the porters' work, he sees that the union allowed the men to take pride in their work, because it provided a structure within which it was possible to challenge the inhumane, demeaning aspects of the job. With the establishment of the union, the men could continue to work without having to passively accept racist abuses. In his words:

To provide a service to a human being does not mean that one lacks dignity, or is an Uncle Tom, or any of these things. The question is: What are the conditions under which those services are being provided? There was a time in the history of this country when black people provided that service on the railroad, and they provided it without dignity. They provided it in an atmosphere where there was no organization that allowed them to challenge the circumstances, the conditions under which they could provide those services or not provide those services. So, the evolution of the development of that union gave, it seemed to me, the same kind of pride to black people. That is, the ability to organize, the ability to struggle on their own behalf, the same kind of thing that I've got from my uncle and my father and my family in terms of the need to focus in on issues and challenge on behalf of those issues. So, I see the development of the Brotherhood of Sleeping Car Porters as an extraordinary moment in the history of this country. It was the first black trade union that allowed people to understand that in organization there was strength—they could develop the capacity to challenge on their own behalf and to direct destiny based on their input rather than someone else's manipulation.[44]

Although Dellums eloquently separates servile work from the intrinsic worth and value of the worker as a social being and a human being, porters had to work this out for themselves. Working under the conditions they did, constantly being told they were inferior (and in fact always treated as such), working a job that was based on a social structure that reified race as a determinant of personal worth, porters struggled to maintain their sense of self-worth, to keep their occupational identity discrete from their personal identity. In short, they needed to convince themselves that they were not being Uncle Toms as they worked a service job. The union and A. Philip Randolph helped. So did the sharing of experiences with other men, through the telling of occupationally related anecdotes, personal experience narratives, and stories traditional to their occupational and ethnic cultures. It is through this occupational folklore that porters, then and now, established, declared, and maintained their identity and reconciled the many contradictions they faced daily, throughout their years. In later chapters, these narratives will be examined in depth. Now, however, this chapter will close with a summary statement by William Harrington, reflecting on his life:

> After Randolph *made* the job I enjoyed it. And I enjoyed it ever since I retired. I enjoyed my retirement. Now I don't want to hear a train whistle blow. It was a good job after we got an agreement with the Pullman Company, but before we got an agreement, it was hell on wheels. The best thing that ever happened was when I could make a decent salary and make a decent living to take care of my family. That's the best thing that ever happened to me. And that didn't happen until after the agreement was signed with the Pullman Company.
>
> When I couldn't make ends meet, that was the worst thing. That was the worst thing. That's when I was young and couldn't hold a run. I got so I could hold a run, I could take care of my family. That was *after* 1937. We had some kind of recognition. We were recognized. Before that time nobody recognized the porters but passengers. Our passengers gave us more recognition than *some* people.
>
> That's about my life.[45]

NOTES

1. William H. Harris, *Keeping the Faith: A. Philip Randolph, Milton P. Webster, and the Brotherhood of Sleeping Car Porters, 1925–37* (Urbana: University of Illinois Press, 1977), 89–107.

2. Ibid.

3. C. L. Dellums, November 13, 1980.

4. See Jervis Anderson, *A. Philip Randolph: A Biographical Portrait* (New York: Harcourt Brace Jovanovich, Inc., 1973) for a full account of the life of Randolph.

5. Anderson, 63.

6. Ibid.

7. *New York Times*, May 18, 1979.

8. Harris, *Keeping the Faith*, 30.

9. Harris, ibid., 4.

10. Anderson, *A. Philip Randolph*, 158.

11. Harris, *Keeping the Faith*, 25–41.

12. C. L. Dellums, November 13, 1980.

13. C. L. Dellums, November 16, 1980.

14. E. D. Nixon, July 14, 1981.

15. C. L. Dellums, November 17, 1980.

16. C. L. Dellums, November 13, 1980.

17. See, for example, Anderson, 1973, and Harris, 1977.

18. Fred Fair, March 30, 1983.

19. William Harrington, July 16, 1982.

20. C. L. Dellums, November 16, 1980.

21. Homer Glenn, August 18, 1980.

22. Rosina C. Tucker, June 19, 1981.

23. Rosina C. Tucker, June 6, 1982.

24. Harris, *Keeping the Faith*, 89–116.

25. William Harrington, July 16, 1982.

26. C. L. Dellums, November 13, 1980.

27. C. L. Dellums, November 17, 1980.

28. William Harrington, July 16, 1982.

29. E. D. Nixon, February 25, 1981.

30. William Harrington, May 2, 1980.

31. Lawrence W. Davis, June 27, 1984.

32. A. Philip Randolph, from an audiotape housed at the Newberry Library in Chicago.

33. Rosina C. Tucker, May 26, 1982.

34. E. D. Nixon, July 14, 1981.

35. Rosina C. Tucker, June 1, 1982.

36. E. D. Nixon, July 14, 1981.

37. Ernest Ford, Jr., September 11, 1978.

38. Homer Glenn, August 18, 1980.

39. C. L. Dellums, November 17, 1980.

40. Rosina C. Tucker, July 7, 1984.

41. Leon Long, November 12, 1980.

42. William Harrington, July 16, 1982.

43. Rosina C. Tucker, December 15, 1986.

44. Congressman Ronald Dellums, November 16, 1980.

45. William Harrington, July 16, 1982.

3. A. Philip Randolph
and the Blank Check

Narratives play an important role in the lives of the men who were Pullman porters. Of these narratives, an account of an alleged attempt to buy the allegiance of A. Philip Randolph is frequently told amongst porters (and to outsiders as well) at occasions when porters meet for business or pleasure or both. The stories the porters share are cultural artifacts: they tell us something about the men that tell them, the times of which they report, and the perception of those times by the men who lived in them. The stories are cultural products—different men recount the events in different ways. No one narrative can be held as the single "true" account. Rather, these stories represent truth on a cultural level: the way a group of participants, or actors, interpret the events and times of their experiences. Pullman porters are good storytellers; theirs was and still is (among the retired men today) a primarily oral culture. Making of their past a good, well-performed story is itself a prized activity and a valued capability. It is important that we see the narratives as artistic re-creations. Edward D. Ives has written that the past is everything that ever happened, while history is a selective reading of certain aspects of the past in light of the present.[1] In the porters' narratives, we can see how a cultural subgroup shapes its past into a meaningful, usable history, a body of tradition for the present.

Occasionally, an event and a particular story sum up an entire set of feelings and become symbolic of the group. A. Philip Randolph's resistance of the Pullman Company's attempts to bribe him by offering him a blank check has become such a story. The principles of honesty, integrity, and dignity are epitomized in it. The man could not be bought, bribed, moved, cajoled, threatened, or otherwise corrupted. These qualities are central to the porters' image of themselves.

The story is found in many variations, all of them known through oral tradition. Porter Alan C. Speight refers to it when explaining the union's success as due to having good men and a good man "at the top":

It was a little rough in the first, because they didn't want to talk to us. When we was getting organized, to get Mr. Randolph—to get him to forget that he ever heard about a union or anything—they sent him a blank check, to fill in his amount of money. But he didn't do it. He sent it back to them. . . . He didn't do it, he didn't sell us out. We had a pretty good group—Dellums out in California, same Dellums that's in Congress right now. We had Patterson from the Virgin Islands, Webster in Chicago (he was the chopping man). We really had a bunch of good men. Because at the top we had good men. We had a good man, and he wouldn't stand for that other stuff.[2]

Mr. Harrington claims to have actually seen the check, although this is disputed:

They sent him a check and told him to name it. And he made a photostatic copy and sent it back to them. And during those times, I don't believe another man, a Negro or otherwise, would have done that. Yes sir, he told that several times, and *showed* the check. At the meetings. He made a photostatic copy of the check and sent it back to the Pullman Company. I saw him speaking and he had it in his hand. Yes indeed, the Pullman Company would have bought A. Philip Randolph.[3]

Porter Fred Fair also had a version of the story:

What you heard was true. They went to him twice and offered him some money. I don't know how much money they offered him, but he told them that the Brotherhood wasn't for sale. And the third time they sent an instructor out of New York over to his office with a check. Blank. And told him to put *his* figures on it. And Mr. Randolph took the check and had it photostated, and he sent the check back, and he kept the photostat and framed it and put it in his office. Anyway, he had that check—it's true, he had that check. It's true, he had that check. He wouldn't sign it or accept it. It's framed, it's right in Mr. Randolph's office.[4]

As is obvious from his repeated insistence that the story is true, the story is very important to Mr. Fair. As we look at other accounts, we will see that the details vary from porter to porter, as might be expected, but sometimes the variance is quite significant. The porters often quote Randolph as the source of the story and offer as evidence eyewitness accounts of having seen the check at public appearances that Randolph made. Thus the story, which is a testament to Randolph's honesty, uses Randolph's honesty as proof of the veracity of the story: Randolph himself said it, so it must be true. Ernest Ford says that he heard both Randolph and also his right-hand man, Milton Webster of Chicago, tell of the blank check incident. Therefore, he concludes, the story must be true: "I heard that in his speech from his mouth, that they gave him a blank check. All he had to do was write his figure in it, and I've heard him make speeches time and time again, and this would always come up. Of course, Mr. Webster also made the same statement, and he was there to witness this."[5]

Notice that for Mr. Ford, it is the word that is important, that is, the fact that he heard it "in his speech from his mouth." Not only is the source unimpeachable, as far as he is concerned, but also this reflects the fact that the story is part of an oral culture. Men believe the story of the blank check because they have been *told* it, not because they have read of it. It is the nature of oral culture that details vary in different accounts of the same events, and it has sometimes been confusing to outsiders who fail to understand how different accounts can simultaneously be said to be true.[6] While this story's variations are significant enough to call into question whether there in fact ever was a blank check (C. L. Dellums, who was closer to Randolph than any other man alive today, says he never saw any such check or photostat), the "truth" contained in this story concerns Randolph's character. The stories are metaphorical, although they are quite important and are believed to be true by most of the men.

Homer Glenn, a porter from New York, shies away from claiming to be a firsthand witness to the existence of the check. He also adds a different detail. In his version, Randolph fills out the check in an amount that is unbankable:

> I was in the national office and I had an office in the Brotherhood where Mr. Randolph was, and I had the privilege that I could walk in his office any time. I didn't have to ask to see him or anything. And I was in the meeting, lots of meetings, and it has been said that he'd been offered these checks. The way I heard it he told the Pullman Company that the amount he put on the check was unbankable. There was no bank in the world could cash the amount he put on the check.[7]

Walter Cole, of Chicago, in his version says:

Where I got my news from (this is along about '38), Brother
Randolph was, you know, had a meeting, around Michigan
Avenue. I never will forget this day. And he and about a
hundred of us out there, anyway, we had that flat full. And
he made a talk, and he told the boys . . . "I told the Pullman
Company," he said. "They have made me an offer." And one
of the boys said, "Brother Randolph, can't you tell us
something about it? What is that offer?" He said, "Well, I
just want you to know, they offered to give me a check for
twenty-five thousand dollars. And I refused it. And they
gave me a blank check." They says for him to put what he
wanted on it. And he says he told them, he says, "I don't
want nothing but the porters." And I love that man today in
his grave, because if it hadn't been for him, I wouldn't have
the home I've got in Chicago today.[8]

Note that Cole equates Randolph's honesty and perseverance
with his own economic comfort. He also refers to his story as "news,"
not as a tale; that is, something that he perceives as truth, not
fantasy; something that actually happened, not something made
up. Leon Long also refers to it as "news," although he makes it a
point to mention that he never actually saw the check:

I was in New York about that time, because that's where I
got that news about him having that check and having it up
in his office. He had a blank check, and he wouldn't cash it.
Mrs. Tucker's seen it, but I didn't see it. Around the
quarters a number of people, guys, would be talking about
it, saying, "Who else wouldn't take a blank check and put
the amount of money he wanted on it?" I heard that. I didn't
see it, I heard it.[9]

The least-elaborated versions of this event are usually reported
rather than performed,[10] and the details of the narrative that remain
constant in most tellings are: the company sends Randolph a check
for twenty-five thousand dollars which he refuses. The company
then sends him a blank check, which he can fill out to any sum
he wants. Again he refuses the check. When the porters are socializing, however, each raconteur uses the story as a vehicle for
his own commentary. For example, Mr. Cole sometimes says that
Mr. Randolph referred to slavery by remarking, as he refused the
check, " 'You could buy my parents but you can't buy me.' " In the
rendition quoted above, Mr. Cole said that Randolph's response
was, " 'I don't want nothing but the porters.' "

Other porters tell it in other ways. One man says, "After he refused the twenty-five thousand dollars, the Pullman Company had sent him a blank check and typed on the blank check, 'Honor Up To Six Figures' and told him to just fill in the check, to forget union brotherhood."[11] Some men say he had the check photocopied and displayed it on his desk. Some say he pretended to accept it but never cashed it, instead showing it at Brotherhood meetings as evidence of the Company's duplicity. As mentioned above, C. L. Dellums, who worked closely with Randolph, has never actually seen the check or any photostat of it, even though many men say he kept a copy of it on his desk. One porter, who was himself not in favor of the union, maintains that Randolph pretended to refuse the check, but in fact *did* accept it. This, he says, explains the photostat, because Randolph had cashed the original. But E. D. Nixon emphatically insists that Randolph returned the check:

> After the brotherhood had won the right to organize the porters, the Pullman Company found that they had been defeated. And to make themselves look good, they sent A. Philip Randolph a check, a signed check, and all he had to do was put the amount of money he wanted in the check, and on the bottom it said, "Not to exceed a million dollars." I said it'd be hard to find a man or a woman, or any person as far as that's concerned, who wouldn't have accepted that check and drawn a reasonable amount of money off of it. But Randolph made a photostatic copy of that check, and framed it and hung it on his wall and sent the original back to the Pullman Company and told them Negro principles were not for sale. And he died at the age of ninety years, one month, and one day old. And the last time I remember I saw him, he didn't hardly know who I was. But he is my friend. And he's my kind of man.[12]

Although Leon Long mentioned that Mrs. Tucker had actually seen the check, she herself says only that she, like so many others, had heard about it:

> I can't tell you anymore, than that I understood that Mr. Randolph was followed everywhere he'd go, with the idea of trying to find something on him. I understand—now, I don't know this, but I understand—but it was well published from mouth to mouth that Mr. Randolph was offered this blank check to stop the Brotherhood. That Mr. Randolph, when he traveled, they would send women along to . . . seduce him, I

guess. I don't know if women seduce men or not, but that's the idea. And they never did, you know. But they used many, many ways of trying to discredit Mr. Randolph. Mr. Randolph had an opportunity to get a big government job, but he wouldn't. *He wouldn't be bought.* And that's one thing that made us so successful. And Mr. Randolph was honest and dedicated to this thing, and he carried himself in a proper manner all the way through.[13]

Despite the overall range of the stories—in some he rejects the check, in others he pretends to sign it, and, according to one man, he actually kept the check—the point of the story in the overwhelming number of versions is that he refused the corruption of the Pullman Company, and of the white world in general.

Mrs. Tucker evokes the essence of Randolph's spirit and influence:

And it got to the point where sometimes I was a little discouraged. But I'd call Mr. Randolph and say to him, "Mr. Randolph, how are things coming along?"

"Mrs. Tucker, they are progressing very nicely."

I found out that I was having faith in his faith. That's where my faith derived, from his faith.[14]

A. Philip Randolph was an inspiration to others to continue on. The following chapter will feature stories about the tests and temptations the porters were put to. The story of the blank check provides the porters with a role model of unfailing integrity, and it has become a central narrative, a legend, of porters' experiences. At its core lies integrity. Randolph's heroic deed, the rejection of corruption, is seen as the sine qua non of the Brotherhood's success and is an idealization of the porters' self-image.

NOTES

1. Edward D. Ives, *George Magoon and the Down East Game War: History, Folklore, and the Law* (Urbana: University of Illinois Press, 1988), 3–31.

2. A. C. Speight, July 1, 1982.

3. William Harrington, July 16, 1982.

4. Fred Fair, March 30, 1983.

5. Ernest Ford, Jr., June 29, 1984.

6. See, for example, Albert Lord, *The Singer of Tales* (Cambridge, Mass.: Harvard University Press, 1960) and Barre Toelken, "The 'Pretty Lan-

guages' of Yellowman: Genre, Mode, and Texture in Navaho Coyote Narratives," in Dan Ben-Amos, ed., *Folklore Genres* (Austin, Tex.: University of Texas Press, 1976), 145–70.

7. Homer Glenn, August 18, 1980.

8. Walter Cole, May 18, 1980.

9. Leon Long, July 7, 1982.

10. Dell Hymes, "Breakthrough into Performance," in Dan Ben-Amos and Kenneth S. Goldstein, eds., *Folklore: Performance and Communication* (The Hague: Mouton, 1975), 11–74.

11. Anonymous, 1983.

12. E. D. Nixon, May 27, 1981.

13. Rosina C. Tucker, June 29, 1984.

14. Rosina C. Tucker, November 4, 1982.

4. The Porter on the Train

The triumph of the union by no means eradicated racism or abuses within the structure of the job of porter, certainly not immediately. These difficulties continued to pervade the porters' experiences through the twentieth century, although the existence of the union provided a means for porters to address these problems. Their stories are developed from their day-in, day-out experiences at work on the train and at play during layovers, and can be seen as presentations of incidents that frame strategies they used at different times to deal with various situations. As black male service workers, their position was special. They had to negotiate a wide manner of social and occupational conflicts. Their narratives reflect this and are especially rich. As entertainment, they were primary to their mobile occupational lifestyle. In such a society (marked by travel, movement, new experiences, and exploration of new places) talk was their entertainment, and narratives (stories of personal experiences or stories that they heard and passed on) were essential to this communication. This chapter will survey the situations that these narratives present, examine the narrative structure that underlies them, and suggest ways that the porters used their stories—that is, their culture—to help them deal with their varying situations. The analysis will look back and forth from the social base (status, race, and so forth) to culture, and at the interrelationship of the two.[1]

Rooted in slavery, the narratives share some of the characteristics of blues songs. Like the blues, there is both protest and much raucous, earthy fun in them. As in the blues, people can escape their troubles by having a good time with each other, with a deck of cards, perhaps with a bottle. Since the narratives deal largely with personal experiences, the texts are not as formulaic as the songs, of course, although Barry Lee Pearson has determined narrative patterns similar to those of the porters in his study of the life stories of blues singers and musicians.[2] As in gospel music, there is spiritual imagery: human beings can escape their troubles with the help of God. However, although in blues songs the train is a means of escape and a symbol of freedom (and it was for the young men who became Pullman porters), as they worked, the train became the scene of their troubles.³ The train took them away from mundane life, but it replaced their wanderlust with a new set of problems. The old metaphors no longer worked in the new, complicated reality of the Pullman porters. They needed new symbols, new stories. A. Philip Randolph and the struggle to found the Brotherhood of Sleeping Car Porters provided many of these. The rest were created from the occupational lives of the workers.

The narratives not only protest conditions, they discuss the way to protest, the when and the how of it. These narratives, the folklore of the Pullman porter, are as much a response to stereotyping as unionization was to intolerable conditions. Besides stories of protest and pain, though, there are stories of good times as well. Porters insistently make the point that life on the cars was not all bad, and their story is incomplete without mention of the good times. Happy Davis says, "All work and no play makes Jack a dull boy. You should have seen the porter when he was *playing*. It was *fun!*" Life was not easy, but they did more than survive, more than endure. They enjoyed. There seems to be truth to the idea that richness of experience can be measured by the capacity for depth of experience; that great pain and great joy each allow for the existence of the other in some unfathomable, symbiotic way. That the porters suffered greatly in their time is obvious. Nevertheless, their joy is very much a part of them, and it contributed to their human and historical triumphs. It is what makes them, as men, as charismatic and as vital as they are.

Porters faced dualities every day. It was a good job and a bad job; they were hosts and they were servants; they had the highest status in their community and the lowest on the train. Many more such dualities were part of their everyday work, too, such as good passengers and bad, good conductors and bad, the porters who were brothers and the porters who were Uncles—Uncle Toms.

Whereas in the nineteenth century the Pullman Company hired ex-slaves, in the twentieth century it treated the porter as if he were property. "They considered us part of the equipment," says Ernest Ford. "You see, they treated us like we were part of the equipment. They thought they *owned* us."⁴ This feeling of being treated like someone else's personal property is a central concern of porters, and it is found in their stories. It hearkens back to the days of slavery, when blacks *were* property, and it refers to the porters' daily challenge of providing service, of putting themselves at someone else's beck and call, yet in such a way as to retain their dignity. If the company treated porters as if they were objects it had purchased, too often customers behaved in a similar way. Porters worked for tips: they had to hustle and force themselves to swallow a thousand and one indignities a day and worse. For this they were lampooned as Uncle Toms. They were in a situation with no positive alternatives. It was out of this situation of conflict and cognitive dissonance that they developed their routines, their stylized ways of serving passengers and carrying out their work.

Porters who betrayed their coworkers or bribed administrators to get a better run were considered Uncle Toms, but they were in the minority. Although the porters worked in a job that encouraged competition and individualism, usually they aided each other—for example, covering a fellow porter's car while the man stole a few hours' sleep, warning each other if somebody learned that a spotter was on board, and teaching new porters the tricks of the trade. Leon Long, for instance, reports:

> Why, right here in Washington there were many times I'd have porters get sick, and I'd do the next car next to me. I'd do his work and discharge his passengers. That man told me, "I'm going up to the station, get me some medicine. I don't feel well." We were going to Chicago. And he came back that night before we got to Pittsburgh that night, and he was sick and went to bed, and he had passengers that . . . had to go to bed. I'd finish mine, go up and see about his. At night I'd go up and shine his [passengers'] shoes. He was sick and laying in the smoking room, on the couch. We wired Chicago to have an ambulance meet the train. I'd have the passengers go out my door instead of his door, and I'd discharge all of them. Many times things like that happened. I had two or three porters die on the train, and I'd have to help out and do his work. The man I just told you about died in the hospital. Sometimes they got sick, sometimes they got left. I've been hurt, and porters helped me out.[5]

Porters spent many long hours together, both on trips and on layovers. It was to their advantage to cooperate rather than compete. Moreover, except for the competition for the preferred runs that produced more gratuities, they did not vie for territory or physical space. In contrast, take the case of salespeople for a large department store, who have been described as competing for customers by subtly or blatantly interfering with and sabotaging their coworkers' performances.[6] In the case of porters, territory was very clearly defined, and such problems did not arise: "We didn't have congestion. You didn't bother my stations, and I didn't bother yours," says Ernest Ford.[7]

Tipping was important. Their livelihood depended on it. So the porters thought about it a lot and applied themselves to it, even though they did not compete with each other for the tips of individual passengers. "You had to con a lot of them [passengers], get inside them and make them feel like they were the boss. They *were* the boss. *Everyone* was your boss; that's how we were trained."[8] This comment by Happy Davis indicates a basic tension the porter felt between his realization that although he in fact controlled the car he worked on and so was in charge, he served and took orders from the passenger, so the passenger was the "boss." Nevertheless, the porter ultimately knew that he was in control of his car in many subtle but important ways. When it came to maximizing tips, the porter could manipulate his situation to his advantage.

The coping mechanisms porters developed were similar to those developed by slaves before them, as reflected in the traditional folk narratives often documented in African-American culture. For instance, many of the porters' tales are similar to slave materials such as the "Old Marster and John" stories. In these tales, John the slave usually (though not always) tops or "caps" the slave owner with a display of verbal wit. The struggles the slave faces are social rather than merely physical, and his skills are those of the trickster hero rather than the strongman.[9] In this way, the personal experience stories are very consistent with traditional black folktales. Not only the stories themselves, but also the trickster figure and the narrative structure, were traditional in African-American culture, and therefore culturally available to the porters, who use the stories for similar reasons in similar circumstances.

Happy Davis continues: "A railroad man always had money. I was never broke a day in my life while I was working as a Pullman porter." As evidence, he offers a tale of how a porter once lost his entire paycheck in a card game, and rent was due the next day. Penniless, he left on his run. When he returned, he had enough money to pay his rent. "When a passenger entered my car, I had him. I had ways. I was way *ahead* of them."[10] How far ahead? Beyond special favors and kind words, porters had to apply some psychology as part of their stock repertoire of tricks for getting tips.

Happy remembers the time a rich, elderly lady was traveling on his car:

I had Mrs. Will Rogers, practically on her deathbed. I had to lift her from one bed to another, accompanied by a nurse in the room, and I had to pick her up out of this bed and put her over on this bed, and vice versa, as long as we could keep her comfortable. So on one occasion, while I was doing that thing, she asked me, "Porter, how much do you think I weigh?" She didn't weigh but a feather. I said, "You weigh 135 pounds." So she said, "Thank you!" And when she got off, I got 135 skins! *Beautiful!*

Happy goes on to say:

Railroading was remunerative. You never was broke. You *couldn't* get broke on a Pullman car. Whenever you put your foot on a Pullman car, with passengers you better bet your bottom dollar you've got some new money. It's a wonderful thing, working on the railroad. I enjoyed every minute of it.[11]

Tipping was a central aspect of the job. It made up the major part of the porter's salary. As regards tipping, Mr. Leroy Shackleford of Chicago remembers his first trip:

My first trip was kind of hectic. I made my first trip to Oakland—the first trip by myself. I went to Oakland, California. I was on a tourist car, and I had what they call top and bottom load, you know. I had thirty-two beds, and when I started making the beds, I started about, oh, five-thirty in the evening, because as the sun was going down and the people left the car, I started making the beds. I was making beds until about two o'clock in the morning, see, because I really didn't know too much about it, and when I started making those beds, it didn't look like I was ever going to get through. So I said, when I got back to Chicago, I was going to quit, wasn't going to work this job, because I wasn't doing so well. So then when I got to Oakland and discharged my passengers, and people were coming up and tipping me, you know, I must have made about 75 or 80 dollars. Because when I started I was only making $66.50 a month, so that was an awful lot of money, you know. So that sort of changed my mind. I said, "I'll try to stick it out." And then I started getting a little better. After about six months, I could make a car down in about an hour, which wasn't bad.[12]

And William Harrington comments on tipping as an ironic neces-sity: "We didn't make any money when we made a run unless we made tips. They tell me the Pullman Company had $40 million."[13]

Happy Davis was once visited by an Internal Revenue Service representative who was determined to collect taxes on the tips porters received. She calculated so many passengers per car, so many runs per month, at approximately two dollars' tip per pas-senger, and came to the conclusion that Porter Davis was earning thousands of dollars in unreported income. "*Hold it!*" Happy pro-tested. "Sometimes these cars go out without a single *passenger* on them!" The tips that they acquired as part of their wages could be good, but not quite as good as the IRS or the Pullman Company liked to believe. However, the tips were essential to the porter's livelihood, so he approached his passengers in hopes of the largest possible gratuity. Says Happy:

> I meet a man just like I meet you. When I talk to a man, I'm talking to a *man*. I ain't talking to my superior, I'm talking to a *man*. . . .
>
> I never had any trouble out on the road. I never had one minute's trouble on the railroad with a passenger. Always got the right hand of fellowship. Everybody was glad to see me and glad to leave when they left. I always got shaking hands and hugs and kisses and everything else, you know.
>
> Under some of the *worst* circumstances, I could make a passenger feel good. If he said, "Do so-and-so," I said, "I got that *covered*. I will take *care* of that." I'd say, "This is a shame. This ain't supposed to *be* like this. I'll take care of it right away." And I'd walk away from it. I'd come back and I'd say, "How's everything?" "Everything is fine." I didn't do a *damned* thing! I didn't do nothing. It was strictly confidence all the way![14]

Happy sees his relationship with passengers as essentially equal at the same time that he describes it as a con game ("strictly con-fidence"). In the incident he described earlier concerning Mrs. Will Rogers, he made the passenger feel good, and so she rewarded him with a particularly large tip. Although it can be seen as exploiting an elderly woman, in this case at least, his deception was harmless. Still, it points to the necessarily adversarial, cat-and-mouse rela-tionship between passengers and porters. Conceivably, Mrs. Rogers rewarded Happy for the upbeat message of a scam she never fell for but was flattered by nonetheless. If his story is accurate, we might assume that she knew she did not weigh 135 pounds. Viewed from this perspective, the tip becomes a recognition of a good performance. Performance is intrinsic to the porter's job. While working, he is "onstage." Porters must please their passengers as part of a psychological persuasion; the passengers know this and expect it, and superior performances are recognized.

Among the porters themselves, however, the situation is different. In the 1933 motion picture *The Emperor Jones*, Paul Robeson stars in what is one of the few Hollywood portrayals of Pullman porters that is not stereotyped and demeaning. Playing a young porter on his first run, Robeson sits down to shine shoes with an older, more experienced worker. The senior porter begins the initiation into this occupational culture by explaining to the novice what the various shoes should tell him about how to size up passengers in terms of potential tips. Holding up two pairs of shoes from one berth, one pair male and the other female, he pronounces them a honeymoon couple. Picking up a somewhat worn, dilapidated shoe, he says, "You'd be lucky if you could shine a dime out of that. But *this*," he enthuses, holding a handsome shoe, "man, this is good for a *half*."

This scene is not too far from real life. Shining shoes has always been one of the most standard activities of the porters, to the point that the image of a porter shining a shoe has become an almost iconic representation of Pullman porters. Surprisingly, however, porters were never actually *required* by the Pullman Company to shine shoes; and for that reason, porters had to buy their own supplies to do so. That they were *expected* to shine shoes is evidenced by the special shoeboxes the company installed in all its cars. Porters wanted to shine shoes, then, insofar as it was a means of getting tips. William Harrington, when asked if he considered the shoe polishing in any way demeaning, equated it directly with tipping: "Well, sure, we shined shoes, but see, I'd shine your shoes, I'd get a *tip* for that. If you didn't tip me, and I caught you again, I ain't going to shine your shoes."[15] Again, tipping is seen by the men as payment for services rendered. Leon Long echoes Mr. Harrington when he describes shining shoes as a strategy, along with brushing a man's jacket, for encouraging a good tip:

> Shining shoes. That was a big part. They didn't pay you
> to do that, but that was where you get your money. You
> shine his shoes, he feels cheap if he ain't going to give you
> anything for it. So you're going to shine his shoes, and
> you're going to be sure to see when he gets off. You've got
> your whisk broom the next morning if he wants to be

brushed off, his shoes already shined, so quite naturally when he walked out, he was sure to give you something to show that he appreciates your shoeshine. Yeah, we'd be sure to have polish. If you're running out of polish, next station you get off and go hunt some. You want to make sure the next morning the man don't walk off and don't give you nothing.

Some of them put on the shoe and find out they've got on the wrong shoe. Yeah, I've seen that happen. Not often, though, because it's just like clockwork when you get into it. You know how many beds you got the shoes from, and you go back in the smoking room and sit down there, and you put them down and go back and get some more. Lots of times you had a pencil, and you mark it on the bottom of the shoe.[16]

Like tipping, shining shoes was very much a part of the porters' daily lives. As such, they developed occupational tricks and ways of facilitating the handling of this chore, like marking the soles of the shoes with the number of the berth they came from. This way, porters could take many pairs of shoes and shine them at the same time and still keep them straight. Inevitably, however, the shoes were sometimes lost or misplaced. Many stories deal with shining shoes, keeping track of them, and losing them. This is another area where stories are representative of the experiences of the group and can be said to accurately reflect a recurrent aspect of the job.

I was once at a meeting of retired porters in New York. It was the first time I had attended. In the course of meeting and interviewing several men, I asked about shoe shining. One man told me how porters were not supposed to shine more than one pair at a time, but that most porters circumvented this difficult rule by marking the soles and taking several pairs of shoes with them into the men's lounge to work on them. This man went on to tell me of an instance when he once took a sack full of shoes into the men's lounge, and while he was in there, during the night, his car was cut out of the train. The passengers of an entire Pullman car were doomed to awaken to a shoeless morning.

After he told his story and we finished talking, the very next porter I spoke with told me the identical story, only he told it as having happened to him. While it is possible that the same thing did happen to both men—and the possibility that it could have happened gives the story relevance—I doubt that in fact it did. Rather, I think we have in this case examples of two folkloristic

processes concerning traditional narrative. The first is the person-
alization of a story that one has heard told; that is, retelling a narrative in the first person as if it actually happened to the narrator.
Many of our best and most famous raconteurs practiced this regularly, including the legendary backwoodsman Davy Crockett and
"Honest Abe" Lincoln himself.[17]

The other phenomenon is simply the gentle hazing of the in-
quisitive outsider, taking him for a ride until he learns the terrain
well enough to know he is being driven in circles. So these stories
may or may not have actually happened to the men who reported
them. However, shining shoes was an economic necessity, and the
porters needed to maximize the numbers of shoes they shined. The
company rules made this difficult, even though the company certainly expected the porters to shine the customers' shoes. C. L.
Dellums explains: "The passengers at night, if they wanted their
shoes polished up, they'd stick them in the box, and there's a door
to it out in the hall. So the porter from the outside, then, could
open that box and get the shoes, shine them up, and put them back
in the box. However, the Pullman Company wouldn't even furnish
the polish."[18]

Happy Davis also has commented on the way the Pullman
Company tried to play both sides of this issue, by assuming that
porters would shine shoes but not requiring them to. This is made
possible by the fact that their salaries were low, and they depended
on tips to make a living. The company knew that their dependence
on tips would ensure that porters would shine shoes so as to increase the amount they might receive from the passenger. Davis
says:

> A porter would shine a man's shoes during the night.
> On one occasion, a porter went to pick up a man's shoes in
> the old cars, under the berth, and he reached down to pick
> the man's shoes up. The man reached out—SLAP!—and said,
> "Uh-oh, no you don't, they's mine!" The man grabbed the
> cat by his hand and said, "Look man, don't you touch them!
> They're mine." He thought the porter was trying to swipe
> his shoes.
>
> Now, just because we make it such a practice, to shine
> shoes . . . meant a little extry tip. Whereas a passenger
> would tip you a quarter, if you shined his shoes he'd
> probably give you fifty cents or a dollar. Now, it got so
> prevalent that we would shine shoes until they put this box
> in the car. They didn't say you had to shine them, but, uh, it

was sort of halfway. They would ask you the question as to whether you shined shoes or not, did you have any qualms about shining shoes. And if you had qualms about shining shoes, you hardly got a run on those regular trains, see?

The stories deal with this situation, in one way or another, and are truly representative of group concerns. Officially, shining shoes was supposed to be a matter of personal discretion, but in reality it was not. What to do when you must shine as many shoes as possible but you are not allowed to? What happens if you break the rules? What are the risks? Happy goes on to tell how a porter took off his own brand-new pair of shoes and had them confused with a passenger's. The poor porter was never to see his new shoes again:

> I'm going to tell you another story, another funny story, about a hard-luck porter. This porter got on the train; he had on a pair of brand-new shoes. Naturally he couldn't work in those shoes, so he took his new shoes off and put on his easy walkers. Now, he changed clothes in the drawing room, so he left his shoes up in the corner. So during the course of the night, the drawing room passengers got on. He made his beds, and left his shoes in the room. It's customary that a customer or a passenger would set his shoes outside the room at night, and you would shine them and set them back. The passenger knew the shoes weren't his, so he set them outside the door. So the porter picked the shoes up, he shined them, set them back down by the door absent-mindedly, and he called the man the next morning to get off. He looked down on the floor, and the shoes were still sitting there. He said, "Hey, mister, I called you. Aren't you up yet?" The man said, "I'm ready to get off, porter." He said, "Well, you left your shoes out here." "Did I?" He reached out and got the shoes, picked them up, put them in his bag, and got off. The porter didn't have no more new shoes. That's the truth. That's the *truth*. That's absolutely the truth.[19]

Fred Fair tells about the problems of dealing with shoes:

> Whether it's true or not, there was a story told on the porter, about taking the shoes to the next car, sitting down with this porter in the next car. But something happened one night and they cut the car out, and this porter had all the man's shoes back in the other car. But I don't know how

true that was. But I had a pair mixed up on me once. I was coming from Atlanta, and I only had them from one berth, one section, but there was upper and lower. And these two men were about the same size boot and their shoes were black. So I took those two pair out and cleaned them and took them back. And the next morning, just before we got into Washington here, well, one of the men said—they were both sitting there talking to each other there in tl e smoking room, and one of them said that he had a little thing in his shoe, the instep, and he had on the other's shoes!

I used to take a pencil and mark them, like most of the porters did, take three or four pair and mark them when we had a chance to do it. I'd always take a pencil and mark them real good.[20]

Homer Glenn, like the other porters, alludes to the truth or possible lack of it in some of these twice-told tales, and he also mentions the porters' custom of marking the soles of the shoes:

I've seen, I've known cases where porters would take a linen bag and just go get all the shoes and put them in the linen bag and go into the next car with the other porter and talk to him and shine the shoes. I heard of an incident, and I am pretty sure it was true, that this porter (you got cars to Buffalo and cars to Detroit and cars to Chicago on certain trains, like the Iroquois 59 out of New York) . . . one of these porters seemed to have taken all of his shoes in his car in one bag and took them up to the next car to shine them and talk to this porter. He found out later that the other cars were cut off from his in Buffalo, and he had all the shoes. But it was just fortunate that his car was going on, and the Buffalo car was sitting there, and he had time to get back over on his car.

It didn't happen to me, because I carried a marker with me. And if I had shoes under A or in B or C, I'd mark each on the sole of the shoe, A, B, or C, or whatever it was, if I wanted to shine more than one pair of shoes. And this way I could keep a straight line where they went. A lot of fellas just took two or three pairs of shoes, and after a while they'd just be shining shoes and somebody'd come and talk with them, get their minds off them, and they wouldn't know where they went. They'd just set them under any bed. But you could easily get them; as long as you were on your own car, you could easily straighten the shoes out.[21]

I wondered if shining shoes presented a problem to the porters, insofar as it was a task they were forced into, both to get tips and to please the Pullman Company. In these ways, it is typical of the job in general, and the two constituencies the porter always had to please. Walter Cole sums up the porters' attitude toward shining shoes: "Shining shoes was not Uncle Tomming. Uncle Tomming was in the way you talk to a passenger, all that bowing and 'yassir' and 'nosir' and all that stuff. Why, you're talking to passengers in a different *tone*. You get on like they were your father, and you were actually afraid of them."[22]

Porters shined shoes to get tips, and even though there are problems intrinsic to the tipping system, the stories are often funny. To porters, getting tips represented a kind of triumph over the system that shackled them. The bigger the tip, the greater they considered their victory. Other ways of getting tips also sparked stories, and these, too, are funny, as we relate to the underdog who wins in the face of adversity. The Pullman porter had to be a trickster to survive; the better the tricks, the stronger the survival. For instance, Ernest Ford says he would prepare for certain trips by researching the areas. He went so far as to learn some French for his trips to Montreal, so he might tell a Canadian passenger that he was a French-speaking Creole from Louisiana, thus fascinating the passenger no end and ensuring a healthy gratuity.

Rich people, politicians, and celebrities rode the Pullman cars. If asked, the porters will recite the litany of famous, near-famous, and once-famous names of people they have carried. Being a Pullman porter brought them into contact with a class of wealthy white people who would not otherwise generally associate with blacks (except as domestic servants). Porters enjoyed hobnobbing with the rich and famous, as anyone would. Green Glenn, the "piano-playing porter," as he was known to his peers, tells of sitting around the piano long into the night with Duke Ellington and other jazz greats. Serving the rich and famous did not always pay off, however. Porter Clarence Talley remembers attending J. D. Rockefeller and receiving only ten cents for his labors. "He only tipped me a dime. It was a very shiny dime, though."[23]

Good humor is typical of the tone taken in reminiscence. One of Ernest Ford's favorite stories involves his *misreading* of a passenger and the situation. The story is interesting because, among other things, he refers to many details of a porter's life: the "weaving and bounding" for tips, the job duties, both technical and personal (i.e., taking care of the dog). Of particular interest are his comments "workers get together" and "workers talk, you know," which indicate a period of nonperformance, a backstage situation,[24] in which workers banter with peers of their own class and occupation, and comment on the superordinate class they serve. Ultimately, the story is about the porters' expectations of and relationship to the larger world:

That was very embarrassing to me, because, you see, I was running on a top train, the Silver Meteor, from New York to Miami, one playground to another, you know? And I picked this passenger up at New York—no, it was Philadelphia. They didn't have but one bedroom and a lot of bags. It was a white lady and a colored lady. Well, the white lady had a little poodle in her arms and was directing me and the Red Cap as to what to do with the bags. So I told the Red Cap to put them all in the room and we'd get it straight once we get on the way.

Well, the white lady was doing all of the ordering around while the colored lady was just going along with her, and I thought this colored lady was the maid, you know. Her name was Mrs. Schwartz; I never will forget it.

This was on the sleeping lounge of which I was operating, and I knew I had somebody because they had a poodle. This was when we could ride with our animals on the car. With all the bags in the room, there wasn't a lot of room in the sleeper, because you're supposed to check them in the baggage car. But all of this is part of my work in trying to make people happy and trying to make a little money for myself. So once we got on the way, they were through with the Red Cap, and I asked the Red Cap, "How were they?" This is our lingo, one worker to another. "How were they?" He shook his head at me, you know [laughs].

I go back to the club car portion of my car where the maid is sitting out there drinking a Coke and, well, workers get together, you know, so I said, "How does the lady treat you? Does she treat you all right?" She said, "Oh yes, yes, she's very nice." Then I said, "Well, that little dog, usually they have the maids with the dog." "Oh no, she keeps the dog real close to her," she tells me.

The next day we're coming into Hollywood, Florida, where they were getting off, and finally she said, "Well, you can get our bags now."

The bags didn't have a name on it, and I took them all out except one little handbag that the maid was carrying. I kept weaving and bounding, and I said, "Is there anything else?" Nobody has greased the palm *yet*, you know [laughs]. "Is everything all right?" I said, you know. I opened up the door, I let them know everywhere that they could walk the dog. The only thing I sold them was a Coca-Cola, then I served another Coca-Cola. She gave me a dollar, said to keep the change. So the maid was all right with me, but Mrs. Schwartz hadn't come through *yet* [laughs].

So, to my surprise, I finally got the little bag, because I felt sorry for the maid, and I was mad as heck at Mrs. Schwartz, because Mrs. Schwartz hasn't said nothing, and now the trip is over and she *still* hasn't said nothing. So. I finally got this little handbag from who I thought was the maid and it had a name on it: Ella Fitzgerald. Now, all day and all night I rode with her, and I didn't recognize Ella Fitzgerald![25]

If we examine this story as an expressive artifact of porters' culture, as a thing made by an individual giving intangible but real narrative shape to his experiences, it is quite apparent that the joke is on the porter, who assumes that the black woman is a maid. Ella Fitzgerald is an unusual individual, of course, as a successful black woman who rode the Pullman cars. Mr. Ford would in other cases be correct to assume that the white woman was the boss. In this case, however, we have a comedy based on error. The porter talks to the woman as if she is a peer, but she is not. The story, by reversing the usual reality, throws it into relief and sharpens its focus. The narrative derives from one porter's personal history, but it is told to other porters who relate to it their own experiences, and in their own ways, help shape it.

In telling stories about passengers, the Pullman porter is speaking from a unique vantage point: he worked in one of the few jobs, if not the only job, in which a black male had access to and a view of the white world.[26] Black women, as domestics, witnessed certain white lifestyles, but black men were not allowed intimacy or proximity with white people in large numbers due to *de jure* segregation in the South and *de facto* segregation in the North. As a porter, however, he often was friend and confidant to a class of wealthy white passengers, and at the very least, he witnessed their behaviors, their sins and indiscretions, and sometimes, their tragedies. Because of the stratification in society, a wealthy white passenger was not uncomfortable in the presence of a porter, even if involved in an illicit dalliance. For no matter how close the relationship of a porter and a passenger was on the train, whatever the porter witnessed, the passenger knew their paths would not cross when off. In "real life," that is, off the Pullman cars, passengers and porters traveled in very different social circles. Moreover, a porter was expected to be discreet about those occasions when his passengers were not. Rex Stewart of Chicago recalls:

> I had a lady and her children, and she was on her way to a northern town, just across the border with Wisconsin. And I noticed in the course of the night that she had not slept in her bed; she had two lower berths right by the drawing room, so she had spent the night with him in the drawing room.
> In the wee hours of the morning her husband boarded the train at a certain point. I had to get to this drawing room—I realized that she was in there. I finally made an excuse and went in and told them I didn't want to disturb them. And I had the husband sitting in the smoking room on the other car, and I went there and got her out of there and back into her own bed. I saved that family.[27]

But it was not just indiscretions that porters were privy to. Many of life's most private, personal moments, moments of birth and death, occurred in the presence of the Pullman porter. Leon Long approaches this subject in a very interesting way. He equates the intimacy of being present at the death of a passenger to serving passengers in more mundane ways. He recognizes, and appears to disdain, the most servile aspects of his work when he speaks of running errands for passengers, and he equates it with being a maid. Perhaps he identifies service occupations as female. Among the tasks porters must perform for their passengers is caring for them when they are sick, and from this it is a short step to witnessing deaths. Thus, conceptually, this porter categorizes the tending of sick passengers with the other services he provides as part of his job:

> We'd carry the top people back and forth and they'd tip you good. You always knew that you were going to have something at the end of the line. Of course, you had to show appreciation even before you got to that. You got to treat the passenger nice, you got to take care of them. You got to be their nurse, doctor. You got to be the maid. You got to be everything. The errands, if you stop at different towns, different stops, they want you to jump off, run errands for

them, run to the drugstore. You got to run, get something for them, hurry to get back, you know. All that sort of stuff, to try to wait on them and take care of them. You got to be with them when they're sick. I've been with them when their son died. I've been with them when the man died.

I had a lady die on the car. We were coming up from Florida, after they had that big storm there. So she slept in the upper berth. I discharged my passengers in Boston, all but one. The flagman was watching, because I had my stepping box down. And so he came to see, for me to take my stepping box, if I had another passenger in there. So I told him, I said, "There's a lady in there in the upper berth's been sick and I've been calling her trying to wake her up." She never got up. So he went up there, and she was laying there dead.

I had a man sitting up on my car coming from Jacksonville, over here until we got to Richmond. I got ready to put him off in Richmond. He was sitting up in his seat in the daytime. He was dead. Sitting up in the seat dead.[28]

L. C. Richie also witnessed death:

During my experience, as I said before, I ran regular most of the time in these late years, but the time that I ran extra, that was in the thirties. It started in '29 when the stock market broke. And I happened to be on the train that night when the stock market broke in New York. And we had a gentleman on there coming from Buffalo to New York. He got on and he asked me to get him a paper in Syracuse or Rochester, any time during the night that I could get a paper, to come back and wake him up. He wanted to know about it.

So I found out then (I was telling the conductor about it), and the conductor said, "Gee whiz, he wanted you to wake him up?" And I said, "Yes, that's what he asked me to do." He said, "Well, he must be a big shot." So anyway, we checked on him, and he was a manufacturer out of New Jersey going home. And in Syracuse I got the paper for him, about 2:30, 3:00 o'clock, 2:30 or something like that. He thanked me—I woke him up—ah, he thanked me for it.

And of course, get to New York, you know, you wake your passengers up, you got your call card they give you and tell you what time to call them so they'll be ready to get off in New York. And when I got to New York, why, I'd gotten all the passengers; I'd called them all. And I *thought* I heard *him* answer. And all the passengers were off, and I noticed that this room was still, the door was still closed. So I go back in and I knock on this door and I couldn't get the door open, so I called the conductor to come and get the door open, and we finally got the door open, and he was dead. He read—in the paper was about the stock market in New York that had been—and he wrote on the part of this paper to his wife, and he said, "Wife, this is it." That's all he had on the note.[29]

Porters were allowed intimacy and were trusted with the care of children, valuables, and personal secrets, only when the train was rolling. The porter became host and confidant, and whites were willing to suspend their usual social distance only under these circumstances: (1) specifically, that the porter publicly perform tasks that called attention to the subordinate aspects of his position, and (2) generally, that the passenger be in the situation of travel, in motion between the point of departure and the point of arrival, in a time outside of regular, usual social behavior, a time of marginality when a separate set of roles, rules, and expectations are in operation.[30] Once the train pulled into the station, the porter was once again a member of "regular" social life, in which he was treated as a second-class citizen who, ironically, would not be allowed access to the hotel in which the passenger he had spent the previous night consoling had a suite.

Porters repeatedly turn to their relationships with passengers and the sometimes cruel complexities of those relationships for their narratives; the subject is one that continues to feel unresolved for many men today. In the following story, concerning actress Joan Crawford, the porter's gratification comes from the knowledge that he is doing his job well. In no way does it come from the ungrateful passenger. Notice that Mr. Homer Glenn describes himself as a housekeeper as he specifies a fundamental, major dichotomy in the job, that of host versus servant. He was in control of the situation, so he performed his housekeeping duties well, but because of his servant status, Joan Crawford could choose to ignore him and treat him as an invisible man.

Well, Miss Joan Crawford, when she got on the train, she was going to Los Angeles, and I was running from New York to L.A. on the Twentieth Century Limited, which cuts off and hooks up with the Super Chief out of Chicago. And we were late going into Chicago, and she was upset because she had to have her trunks, two big trunks. She had spoken to the conductor and other people and everything, and they said, "We can *not* get your trunks on the train you're going on. You will get your trunks a day later." She was upset. So I asked her, I said, "Well, give me the checks to your trunks." And she wanted to know right away if the conductor's *told* me. Told *her* that they couldn't go, who am I? I mean, in reality, that's what she meant. Anyway, she gave me the checks, and I went and told the guy there at the baggage truck. I said, "Get these two trunks out of the baggage car and put them on my platform." He did that. When they transferred my car over to the Super Chief, I said, "Put these two trunks in the baggage car." And he did *that*. So, all these people that ride these cars through get off at Chicago and meet the train at the other station.

When she came to the next station to get on the other train, she looked at me and said, "Well? Where are my bags?" I said, "In the baggage car." She looked at me. She didn't smile. She didn't say thank you. But I know that she was happy. And that was important to me. I know that she was happy because she had her bags, and I was very well-pleased too. That's our job, is to please the people. Don't worry too much about the officials, please the people. They're the ones that are paying the express.

The porter is the smartest thing on the railroad. Anything you want to do or want to know, see the porter. When you get on that car, he's your housekeeper. The conductors get off along the way. But the porter went all the way. He's your housekeeper.[31]

The above story says as much, certainly, about Homer Glenn, the man who tells it, as it does about porters' culture generally. Working an often thankless job, confronted with self-inflated, boorish people, Glenn finds internal rather than external justification for a job well done. In fact, a great deal of the porters' material consists of personal experience narratives; they comprise data which are personal in nature and which express individualistic concerns, individualistic experiences. These themes can be taken validly as representative of larger group concerns, however, insofar as they are shared with other porters and are used as part of a repertoire of anecdotes that are told on those occasions when porters meet and socialize.

Moreover, as is evident throughout this chapter, these themes are recurrent. Porters tell traditional tales, such as the incident of losing the shoes, along with other bits of railroad lore and jokes. They have their own personal stories to tell to each other, and these tend to be about similar subjects, since the job experiences were shared. This sharing of job experiences forms the basis of the shared identity, their occupational folklife. Their individual stories are unique, but in each group of porters, each has one to tell about tips or shoes or passengers or conductors.

Porters hasten to say that most often, their passengers did not bother them, did not call them "George," did not physically abuse them. Precisely because their passengers belonged to a refined, mannered class of people, most were not rude or boorish, according to the porters' theory. "Old money asks, new money demands," says Ernest Ford. "We learned from them. You could tell a Pullman passenger in the station, by the way he walks, the way he dresses." Homer Glenn says:

> You must understand, in the Pullman cars, we ride the best class of passengers, the best class of people. Pullman people. You take porters that have traveled for a long time, we could stand on the platform of the station and see people coming down. We could tell whether they were Pullman passengers or not. Just look at them and tell. There was something about a Pullman passenger that was different from a coach passenger. You don't find the average Pullman passenger running down to get on the train, or running over people to get on the train. They takes their time. During those days, they were more dignified, the way they carried themselves.[32]

As is true of so much folklore, the boundedness of the group and the deep extent to which experiences were shared leads to patterned ways of speaking and storytelling. Here, the porters repeat themselves almost word for word on this subject of the type of person who rode the Pullman cars. Mr. Richie echoes Mr. Glenn and Mr. Ford:

> You had the elite traveling with you. A porter, after staying on there so long, you could look at a person as he comes down and tell the type he is. You'll know if he's not used to riding first class, and he may have come into some money and now he's able to pay for it—and, of course, he expresses that with demands. Demanding of you this, demanding of you that. But the porter knows how to handle him. And the one who's had it all the time before, he comes down and asks you, "Would you mind doing this for me?"[33]

Porters admired many of their passengers and were proud to be serving "the elite." For instance, Green Glenn rode with great musicians and jammed with them on the piano. It is among his fondest memories of his life on the railroad. Likewise, Mr. L. C. Richie tells a story, similar to that of Fred Fair in chapter 1, about the time he carried Henry Wallace, vice president under Harry S. Truman. Mr. Richie tells the story with respect and sincere gratitude. He appears to have been genuinely touched by the vice president's actions, and he tells the story as an example of one of the best things that ever happened to him:

I got a telegram from the Pullman Company on a Sunday, and I had to be there nine o'clock the next morning. And this telegram said, "You are assigned to a car going to Albany to pick up the vice president and his party, and you'll get your instructions when you get there." So, I went to Albany and I picked up the party; the vice president was on and what-not. Now, this car consisted of six bedrooms and a lounge, and of course, all these bedrooms were taken by the party, and of course, I set up in the lounge. I slept in the lounge. I left there Monday morning with them. We came through Buffalo, all the way into Chicago, all the way into Iowa. He was from the state of Iowa.

Anyway, one night, about the second night, I'm sitting in the lounge, and he came out and set down in the lounge, and we set there. I'm over here, he's over there. So, finally he said, "Porter, what time do you go to bed?" I said, "I don't go to bed." He said, "You don't go to bed?" I said, "No." He said, "Well, how do you sleep?" I said, "Well, I sit here and sleep, and sometimes. . . ." (I didn't want to tell him that during the day, when they are out politicking—I didn't want to tell him that I went in there and slept in one of the beds while they're gone, you know, while they are out campaigning.) So, he said, "Oh, you must have a bed to sleep in, porter." I said, "No, they didn't make room for me on here, only to be on here to work." He said, "Well, listen, we don't know how long we're going to keep the car, maybe a month. How are you going to sleep?" I said, "Just sitting up where you see me now." He said, "Oh no."

The next morning he told the waiters, the reporters. He said, "Now, you will all have to find another place to sleep, because when we leave here, we catch a train. You'll have to sleep in the train, because the porter is going to use that room. The porter's going to use that room." So they did that.

Now, I'm supposed to be in charge of that car, when they hooked me onto the back of a train. The conductor who was on that train, I mean, going through to the West Coast and so on, he would come back and ask me, "Is everything all right?" He'd take the diagram and sign it. Now, I was doing all of the in-charge work and everything, and all he'd do is sign it.

So okay. We were twenty-one days, up and down the state of Iowa. When we got back to Chicago, they disbanded. In the meantime, I told him, now when the Pullman Company finds out I got any sleep, they're going to take the sleep away from me. They're not going to pay me for it. I'm talking about when they didn't sleep, they didn't sleep. I was supposed to get four hours sleep, but they didn't have a place for me and no relief. Extended tour. So, Vice President Wallace said, "You will get paid for all of this. I'll see you get paid for it. Here, when you go to your district, you give your man in charge my card. And in the meantime, I will write him a letter. And if you don't get any results, you contact me."

So, when I went back, they asked me about my time. I told them, I put in time, no rest, no nothing, all the way through. And the assistant there in the office said, "What do you mean, 'no rest'? You must have been sleeping." I said, "You can look at the diagram." That's all they had to go by. On the diagram, every room is taken. Now, where could I sleep? They paid me, but it took a month longer to get it.[34]

For all their bad experiences, porters certainly had some good ones as well. In Mr. Richie's story, the Pullman Company is the adversary, because they did not allow for reasonable sleeping conditions, nor did it pay porters for time they took to sleep. The vice president shows kindness and concern, but although the story is meant to showcase the consideration of a highly positioned man, it also suggests that a porter had to outsmart the Pullman Company in order to simply stay even. The story parallels other porters' narratives in which conductors are anxious to write up a porter and accuse him of some transgression, only to be reprimanded by the prestigious passenger who has become fond of the porter. Such stories are legion. Here is one, told by porter Leon Long:

One conductor, he's the kind of guy, he comes up and wants to be jabbing you in the ribs or something. I told him I didn't care for no playing, and we got into some sort of argument, and I used some kind of word that didn't set good on his stomach, and he wired Jacksonville to have me taken off his train. So, when I got into Jacksonville, they had another porter standing there, and a platform man and a superintendent come down and wanted to know what was wrong with me, and for me to get off the train. They were going to put another porter on the train. And there was a lady on the train, was put on the train in Miami in my car. And they had told me to be sure to take care of this lady, because she practically *owns* the railroad. She's got stock in it or something.

So I knew then I was leaving her, so I went back in the train with the platform man following me to see where I was going. So I went and told her what had happened, and I wasn't going to be her porter anymore. She said to the platform man, "Give me a pencil." She said, "Take this up to the superintendent's office." Oh, he started backing up then, and backing up then. So he went on and told me to come up to the superintendent's office, and "Oh," the superintendent says. "Oh, come on in here and talk. I want to tell you like I tell my porters down here. Let us handle these cases. Don't you try to settle it."

She gave me her card, with her address in New York, and said, "If you hear anymore about this, you let *me* know." He was cooperating. Next time he brought it up, I said I don't want to talk to you. And he never did bother me about it anymore. Oh, there used to be a lot of nice people that got on, lot of beautiful people got on.[35]

Porters respected their passengers and related to them as "first-class" people. On the other hand, relationships between Pullman porters and Pullman conductors were often quite strained. The conductor made roughly twice what the porter made, but feared the porter as a threat to his job. This division was exacerbated by the company's work rules, especially the running-in-charge provision. Whatever the point of view of the company, the running-in-charge rule was an ongoing sore point of contention between porters and conductors. The porters saw it as simply unjust, as a means of forcing them to in effect do the work of the conductor without being recognized with the conductor's status or with equitable pay. Mr. Richie sets forth the porters' perception of the inequalities of this provision:

Now, they had runs, for an instance, out of Buffalo. You were in charge out of Buffalo. The conductor would pick you up at Syracuse. That's two or three hours. In those two or three hours, that's what you would get. In-charge pay, two or three hours, not the whole trip to New York. Just the three hours, or two and a half, or whatever it would be, and see, they'd cut you off. Now, a conductor, where he'd get on and going to New York, or going wherever he's going, he'd get the whole pay all the way through. But they would cut you to two or three hours—and how you have worked, you have done the work! Because you have picked up all the tickets, you've entered all the diagrams, all the diagrams. And all he does is come back and pick up the tickets, the diagrams, and everything, the call cards and everything, and take the money. If you got anything, you sign for it. That's the way they did it, the Pullman porters.

When they say "putting in the diagrams," that means the car was full of people and the car has been sold out. And the porter had done all of the necessary work so far as picking up the tickets, selling the tickets, and all of this. And all he did was turn the paperwork over to the conductor. The conductor got paid for the trip. The porter only got paid for three hours, while he did the work, you see. The porter did the work.[36]

Porters running in charge were resented by conductors because they were doing their work, and the conductors felt their occupational "territory" was being encroached on. Moreover, it became obvious to everyone involved that when porters worked in charge, they were perfectly capable of handling the job of the conductor, even though they were never allowed to actually become conductors until long after the success of the union. The porters knew they were being underpaid compared to the conductors, but running in charge did mean extra pay. Porters wanted equal pay for equal work; conductors wanted to eliminate the use of porters doing the work entirely. The Pullman Company continued the provision because it meant spending less money on wages; tensions grew. The following several stories show, in the porters' words, how they often viewed conductors, and how they felt conductors viewed them. First is Happy Davis:

See, the porter was just part of the equipment at one time. He wasn't even classified as a man. Because the conductor on a train, he was put out there more or less to keep you straight. And half the time when you get back to your district, you were on the carpet, saying a spotter had written you up. But that was the *conductor* that wrote you up, because he didn't like you. If you was all right with the conductor, you were in good shape. But you had to be all right with a Pullman conductor, "Yes, sir," "no, sir" him, maybe even shine his shoes if he put them under his bed.[37]

Hunter Johnson:

I had one little conductor worked out of New York, but he was a southerner. I was in charge from Charlotte down to Columbia and wrote up that diagram and sold a roomette between Columbia and Charlotte. I was in 10 and he was in 9. So, this conductor comes up, and I turned the money over to him, just like the man give it to me: one quarter, four nickles, and five pennies—$8.50, the fifty cents was in change. I give it to him, and he said, "Who wrote this diagram?" I said, "I did." So, when I give him $8.50, we were standing about roomette 3 to the doorway. "If you got to give me a handful of pennies . . ." BAM! He threw all the change right through the door. I said, "Conductor, that's not my money, and it's not yours. But before you get to New York tomorrow morning, the Pullman Company is going to know about this." He went to the locker, got my book and signed it, and slammed the door.[38]

The concept of a porter doing the work of a conductor was more than economically threatening; it allowed a black man to rise above his subordinate status. The provision seems to have struck deep psychological chords of fear and racism in many white men. In 1934, the conductors' union, the Order of Sleeping Car Conductors, applied to the American Federation of Labor for jurisdiction over the porters in a move intended to result in control of the porters.[39] The porters resisted vigorously, and during the battle the conductors' union appealed to ugly racist fears to support its cause. Attacking the in-charge provision, the union claimed that the white traveling public, especially women, were unsafe alone in a car with a Negro porter. By presenting the porter as a potentially dangerous man, possibly even a rapist, the conductors' union was clearly exploiting racist fears deeply rooted in American society. In fact, this was only the negative side of the positive stereotype of the porter as a humble and shuffling servant who longs for guidance from a white man, which the Pullman Company had been perpetuating in its publicity. Both sides of the stereotype were harmful and widespread, and they will be examined in chapter 5. For now, however, it is sufficient to note that this campaign did little to endear conductors to porters, nor did the initial decision of the AFL's Executive Council to award the conductors jurisdiction over the Brotherhood of Sleeping Car Porters. A. Philip Randolph managed to get the action rescinded, but these events contributed to the distrust of the members of the BSCP who had opposed joining the AFL because they felt it was a racist organization.

William Harrington puts it bluntly:

> The conductors was some of the worst sons of bitches there ever was. And I lived to see every *damn* one of them lose their job. Every *damn* one of them. We had some of the nastiest people in the world out there. And me especially, because they didn't want to see me run in charge, take those tickets.
>
> Also, flagmen ride on the rear of the train. I had trouble with this flagman on a train going to Chattanooga, because he didn't want to see me take those Pullman tickets. I had trouble with a flagman running on a train to Rochester. He said to me up in Rochester one night, "What is the fare from here to such and such a place?" He said, "I want to know so I can tell these passengers." I said, "You ain't got no business telling these passengers *nothing*." I said, "*I'm* in charge of this car." And I told the conductor. You know what the conductor come back there and told him? He said, "Don't you touch a *ticket* of this porter. This porter's in charge." The *train* conductor told him that.
>
> And the same thing happened down in Chattanooga, Tennessee. The old flagman there, he rode on the rear of the train, see. That's where my car was. Now, he just didn't want to see me take those tickets and collect this money from here to Chattanooga, from Chattanooga and back, because I'm a *Negro*.
>
> When the Pullman Company turned the cars back over to the railroad, those conductors lost their job. I told them several times, "That's my job. Keep your damn hands off my tickets." I can tell them that.
>
> I'm the first Negro that ran the Pullman car in South Carolina in charge. 1936. I didn't have to go, travel, but thirteen miles in charge. This side of Florence, South Carolina. I had to go ten to twelve miles above Florence from the North Carolina line down to Florence, South Carolina. I was the first porter who carried that Pullman from here to Florence, South Carolina.

When I left Washington, here, I had most of the officials of the RF & P and Atlantic Coast Line officials. Here come the stationmaster, Richmond. He says, "Well, what are you going to do in Florence? You can't take no ticket, you can't run in charge." I said, "Well, the Pullman Company put me here to do it, and if anybody rides this Pullman car, I'm going to take the ticket." "And you're going to get locked up." I said, "Well, the Pullman Company will get me out." I got to Florence four o'clock in the morning. Here comes the stationmaster. "Porter, you can't take no tickets down here." I said, "If anybody gets on this car, I'm going to take it." Here come the Pullman conductor. "Well, I'm going to take this up with my union." "I don't give a damn. I'm going to take those tickets. Now don't come bothering me." The first man from Jacksonville, the first man got on my car, he had a big farm, Barnaby Roach, a millionaire. They only had hunters on this train.

Before I left Washington, I told them, "I don't want this run down South." They said, "Well, you're the only in-charge porter we have." I told them straight: "You know how those white people are down there. They don't want to see you take no ticket," I said, "and I don't want to run." They said, "Well, you just make this trip and come back and tell me." So I decided to make the trip. When I came back, I told him everything that happened. And he made a note of it—his secretary made a note of it—and he wrote a letter down there. And everybody after that was as nice as he could be. Because the Pullman Company would back us up and run us in charge. That's one thing I can say about the Pullman Company.[40]

Several aspects of Mr. Harrington's testimony are striking, not the least of which is the vehemence with which he remembers and discusses the conductors. There is real anger and bitterness here. Moreover, one notices that in each of the anecdotes that Harrington recounts, he casts himself in the role of a fearless hero: one who confronts the conductors, challenges them, and makes them back down. In all the stories in this chapter having to do with the life the porters experienced on the railroad, this issue of confrontation emerges as a central concern of the porters. When to confront and when not to, and to what extent, are issues the porters work out in their occupational narratives, reminiscences, and jokes. Finally, Harrington's words end on an ironic note: he credits the Pullman

Company for backing him up and for running him in charge in the first place. This reflects the fact that life itself is always complex, and situations are never simple. Conductors could be quite nasty, as we have seen, but the situation was one of paradoxes and dualities. Obviously, there were kind and sympathetic conductors as well as cruel and racist ones. For instance, in another situation in which the train had stopped in a small southern town known for its prejudices, a conductor volunteered to go and get food for the porters. He warned them not to go by themselves, saying, "In this town they don't even have black chickens."

So, there were good and bad conductors, despite the porters' overall view of them as bad. Likewise, there were good and bad passengers, even though porters have generally good things to say about the people who rode their cars. Despite their overall respect for, and even identification with, their passengers, porters tell many stories of heartbreaking humiliation. Indeed, the porters' views and interpretations of the social class they served, and their relationships with that class, constitute one of the most pervasive themes of their stories.

Mr. Ford tells of the time he had the Duke of Windsor on his car, and of the many special services and chores he rendered the Duke. Every time he did something, the Duke gave him a dime, a "silver offering," as Ford called it. By the end of the trip, Ford had been given eight dimes but had spent three of them. As he looked at the coins, he thought, Is this my trip? Five dimes? Then the Duke of Windsor approached him and asked for the dimes back. Mr. Ford gladly returned the five coins. The Duke took the coins and handed porter Ford five new ten-dollar bills. In this story, Mr. Ford was finally given a good tip, but he was put through psychological torture to get it. He was demeaned, humiliated, and reminded of his lowly status.

Green Glenn reports a comparable kind of passenger:

We had one classification of tippers that were known throughout the Pullman Company. At one time or another most all Pullman porters ran into them. They were this class that would get on the train, take a five- or ten-dollar bill, tear it in half, give you one half, and he keeps the other. That was to ensure that you give him good service. You're going to give him all the service you can to get that other half. So you had that class.[41]

Tipping is a part of a complex web of associations that has at its center the institution of slavery, from which the earliest Pullman porters were drawn. W. D. Miller explicitly ties the two together at the end of this story in which he, too, is humiliated but well remunerated. He tells of a passenger who asked him to come to his private berth. The passenger was crying, obviously upset, and needed someone to talk to. He was also self-conscious about the condition he was in, and continually asked Miller if it were all right to be talking to him like this. Every time he asked if it were all right, he handed the porter a tip. "It's my daughter," the passenger says, still in tears. "You don't mind my talking about it?" He tips the porter. "No, of course not. What about your daughter?" "She ran away to New York. Are you sure you don't mind my talking about it?" he says, as he hands the porter another tip. The story gradually unfolds. The man's daughter has run away to New York to get married. "What's so terrible about that?" the porter asks. "You should be happy." "No," he answers. "She married a Pullman porter!"[42]

Mr. Miller goes on to say that this entire episode must have cost the passenger fifteen dollars in tips. "That's another way of making money without selling yourself," he says, sensitive to the entire tipping system. But look at what he gave in return for that money: time, attention, consideration, sympathy—yes, all of these, but also much more. The story shows the porter as a confidant, a role he was often asked to play. He is subject to humiliation, asked by an insensitive but superordinate passenger to accede to the position that it is tragic that his daughter married a Pullman porter. The only revenge for these indignities that the porter has is to collect the tips as a kind of payment. In other tellings of this story, Mr. Miller quotes the passenger as saying, "She married a nigger!" which makes the story perhaps less job-specific but shows the passenger's behavior to be more explicitly insensitive and demeaning.

Although the porter was recompensed in tips, it was the tipping system itself that allowed passengers to be so rude and insensitive to porters in the first place. If he had not depended on tips, the porter would not have needed to put up with such behavior. The line between selling oneself and maximizing tips—that is, between slavery and economic freedom—was very thin. Perhaps it can be seen as one of the porters' finest achievements that they walked this delicate tightrope with grace. It was a line that the porters were constantly aware of and always attempted to maintain. Whether they were always successful is something that they work out with each other, and internally, in the solitude of their own thoughts.

The specter of slavery is not a mere metaphor or image by which porters compared themselves to the past. The issue is quite real to them, as it was real to A. Philip Randolph and to the management of the Pullman Company as well. By a peculiar twist of fate, the president of the company for a time had been Robert T. Lincoln, the son of Abraham Lincoln. The company sought to exploit this connection, insisting to its porters that it was inconceivable that the son of the Great Emancipator could or would act in any way detrimental to their best interests. In a pamphlet from about 1926, entitled *The Pullman Porter, the Benefits of His Racial Monopoly*, it was written: "It is a fitting coincidence that Robert T. Lincoln, the son of the Great Emancipator, should have been associated with the Pullman Company as general counsel, President, and Chairman of the Board and even now, despite his advanced years, as director."[43] A. Philip Randolph responded to the pamphlet as follows:

> It is unfitting, though interesting, to note how the Pullman Company is desperately trying to make a case for the wages and treatment it now gives the porters and maids by sentimentally appealing to the name Abraham Lincoln through his son. It is a most unhappy and pathetic gesture, for Abraham Lincoln freed Negroes from economic exploitation as *chattel slaves*, whereas his son, Robert T. Lincoln, has lent his influence and name to the notorious exploitation of Negroes as *Pullman slaves*.[44]

It is in the context of this very real awareness of the slavery issue that Pullman porters' narrative, especially that which deals with temptations, tests, and honesty, must be viewed. As in the case of W. D. Miller's stated recognition of the relationship between taking tips and selling oneself, porters were acutely sensitive to the fact that tipping (the arbitrary monetary evaluation of the value of their labor) too closely resembled slavery (the arbitrary economic evaluation of the value of life). The need was to maximize tips yet retain dignity; to do without selling oneself. A. Philip Randolph was a heroic model in this regard. Typical of the interaction between personal and group identity is what Marisa Zavalloni terms "affective identity resonance," whereby characteristics associated with the group become identified by the individual as consonant with his own aims and goals, and positive traits associated with the group can be internalized as belonging to the individual, because the individual belongs to the group in question.[45] Since porters were considered honest and dignified, individual porters considered themselves to be validated as being honest and dignified because they were Pullman porters. A. Philip Randolph repre-

sented the porters (literally and as a symbol); he displayed remarkable honesty and courage; therefore, the porters could assess
themselves as sharing in those characteristics; they could, as Rosina
Tucker said, take strength from his strength.

Randolph's honesty and integrity were repeatedly put to the
test, and these are the qualities that porters cite when speaking of
him. Just as he refused to accept the blank check, porters repeatedly
proved their own honesty, to themselves and to the company which
they often claimed tried to entrap them. New York porter Samuel
Beasley tells of one such occasion:

> One time the president of the Pullman Company left two
> rolled-up dollar bills out, just to test me. But porters are
> honest. Another time a passenger from Canada brought one
> thousand dollars in, but he *lost* it. He didn't report it. He
> was *afraid* to report it. He wasn't supposed to bring that
> much money *into* the country. But I found it, and *I* turned it
> *in*. If I hadn't turned it *in*, he would never have got it,
> because he never would have *reported* it.[46]

Honesty is a characteristic that porters repeatedly point to as
a matter of occupational and personal pride. They mention it frequently, and it is a recurrent theme in their conversational and
personal experience narrative. Fred Fair, for instance, tells an in-
triguing anecdote about a friend of his who found a passenger's
valuable ring but did not recognize its actual worth:

> A friend of mine that worked with me on the President's
> car, he went to Louisville, Kentucky, to the Derby. Only had
> one room and nobody else in his car, so he was complaining
> going down that he wasn't going to make any money.
> Course, he had nobody to make it off of but this lady in the
> room. So, when we got there, she, uh, she lost a ring. And
> he found her ring, and the ring was so big, he just figured it
> was a toy or something, and he threw it up in the locker,
> and then when he went to the office, he took this ring to the
> office, the Pullman office. Well, about six months later, they
> called this man in New York and gave him a check for one
> thousand dollars. The lady was from Wilmington, one of the
> rich people out of Wilmington. But what had happened, this
> ring—I don't know the value of that—but the insurance
> people gave him the one thousand dollars because he found
> the ring. But he got the biggest tip that I ever heard of in the
> service.[47]

This story is interesting. The porter in the story receives his biggest "tip" through his honesty. Even though the porter wanted and needed money (for the Derby), he does not keep the ring. True, he thinks it is a toy, but that does not mean it would have been completely without value. Ironically, he received his unusually large tip for a trip he thought would not be remunerative, but he received it six months later, not in time for the Derby. It is a case of delayed reward, of good things coming to one who waits patiently. Mr. Fair is telling a story here about a porter's honesty, as well as about patience.

It is worth pointing out here that these narratives constitute artistic re-creation and interpretation of past events. In that regard they are the creation of a culturally selective past and a meaningful universe in which retired porters operated more recently. It is not possible to insist on the literal truth of each recounting; obviously, there were dishonest porters as well as other exceptions to the standards that have been so far presented in the porters' words. My intention is not to blur the distinctions, but rather to examine the ways people create a meaningful past, in this case through oral narrative. What is important from this perspective are the values and themes they themselves frame as meaningful. Consistently, porters' stories, such as the two below by Hunter Johnson, showcase honesty:

> I was accused of two rings once. A lady got up and went to the washroom and said she left them on the pillow. I stripped the bed, put it away. She came back and said, "Porter, where's my ring?" I said, "I haven't seen no ring. You didn't leave no ring here." I said, "Check yourself, see if you didn't put them in your bag or something." She said, "No, I put them right here on the pillow." So I just turned to the conductor, and we were leaving Raleigh, North Carolina. So, they just put off a wire for Hamlett, have police come in. Two women and one man, they came down there, take this lady in the washroom, open her bag—there was a stocking tied up in her socks. And she said [the rings] weren't valued at that much. I think one was fifteen hundred dollars, the other nine hundred. So, they come back and told me, "Porter, we found your rings. You didn't have them." I said, "Thank you."
>
> Then I had a man accuse me of stealing a pack of cigarettes. I said, "Mister, I can give you more cigarettes than you be able to buy," because soldiers used to get them

at the PX and sell them to me, fifty cents a carton. He found them down beside the seat. I told him, said, "Mister, the Pullman Company don't have no rogues out here. We weren't hired as rogues, we were hired to *protect* your stuff."

We used to have shoe locks on the new-style cars. You open them from the hall, for getting people's shoes out, to shine them, put them back in there. So one night I picked up a pair of shoes. I looked in them. There was a shoe full of twenty-dollar bills, four hundred and eighty dollars. About two-something in the morning. I went straight to that door and knocked on that door. I said, "Here is your shoes and your money." I said, "Don't ever leave your money like that." I says, "If people come through here and look in that locker and find that money, they'd blame me for it." Because I'm supposed to see everybody that goes through here. And I could be in the toilet, anywhere.

My instructor told us: "No women, no drinkin', and no stealin'." That was it.[48]

Although the company might leave money lying around to see if the porters would take it, or plant bottles of liquor in accessible places to test the porters, they resisted. The stories they tell show that honesty is of utmost importance to them. "The Pullman Company don't have no rogues out here." "Negro principle is not for sale." Their stories have morals, often explicitly stated in the narratives, such as the stories by Hunter Johnson. Further, honesty begets dignity, another quality the porters cherish, and another aspect of their lives that was challenged daily, by being called "George," by being rendered anonymous, by being intimidated and sometimes physically abused. In one case a passenger, who was drunk, kicked a porter. The way you handle a drunk passenger, porters explain, is to make him drunker. You do not jeopardize your tip if you can help it. You may have to rationalize the actions of the drunken passenger, as well as your own responses to him. In such situations, there is always a tension between two roles: porter as servant and porter as man. The dichotomy is one the porters themselves have suggested, "man" here being a socially defined term involving self-esteem, dignity, courage, and so forth. Throughout their careers, porters had to negotiate this duality within themselves, often taking refuge behind the anonymous mask of "servant," because if the porter reacted personally, as a man, the results might prove unfortunate for all concerned. Each porter, in each individual situation, had to decide at what point he would shed his servant identity and react as a man. The servant-man duality was suggested by Homer Glenn, as he explores it in the following story-within-a-story:

> I had a man from Texas once who got in my car. And he went to the club car and he got pretty full. And I was back in the smoker, trying to shine shoes, and he came back with all kind of stories about . . . he had a Negro mammy and he loved black people. He worried me so—I'd go out and get shoes and come back, and he'd still be there. So he worried me so much, finally he said, "You know that it's a shame the way these Negroes rape these people, isn't it? What you think should be done to them?" About that time I was filled up. I says, "Pardon me, do you wish me to answer you as a servant, or answer you as a man?" He said, "Answer me as a man." I says to him, I says, "Sir, in the Negro race, they can get a woman as black as a shoe, they can get a woman as green as an olive, they can get a woman as white as a white woman." I said, "But in the white race, I never see a black white woman." I said, "Now ask yourself the question. Who is the rapist?" "Aw, I think I'll go to bed." He resented it, and he got up and went to bed. He walked off.[49]

This narrative is complicated. According to it, the reason you find so many gradations of color in the Negro race ("black as a shoe, green as an olive, white as a white woman") is because of the "intermingling" of whites and blacks that occurred to a large extent during the days of slavery, when white slave owners sexually assaulted the black women they owned. Glenn's perception, and it is widely shared among porters whom I have spoken with, is that slavery is the primary context that frames many contemporary situations: slavery was cataclysmic and is all-pervasive. Porters, whose jobs were originally held by freed slaves, saw it as the genesis of many of the problems they faced during their lifetimes. Thus, Glenn's remark, "You never see a black white woman," refers to legal and cultural categories. Black ancestry, no matter how limited, is viewed by white society as polluting and places an individual socially as a Negro. That is why one never sees a "black white woman"; culturally there is no such thing.

In the narrative structure of Glenn's story, a story about the servant-man issue frames the story that deals with rape and racism historically. The larger point of the story, for the context in which it was told, is that the passenger said it would be appropriate for Mr. Glenn to answer truthfully, that is, as a man, but in fact, when he did so, the passenger did not like the truth and resented Mr. Glenn for telling it. Glenn's story recapitulates a battle of attitudes and ideas, and status relationships, wherein words were the weapons. The passenger gave Glenn permission to step out of his occupational role, a right that the passenger, in his superordinate position, could confer. However, subordinates are never supposed to step out of their servant roles in reality; the passenger did not expect that he would. By doing so, Glenn actually made sharper the social and status distinctions in operation on the train.

Glenn did win a momentary victory by telling his story. The passenger was embarrassed and retreated. As men of words, the porters were good at using stories to rhetorical purpose. In terms of other social and symbolic battles on the train, they could resist bribes and temptations; drunks they could finesse. They saw their jobs as containing this element of struggle, of maintaining constant vigilance against forces who would see them demeaned and brought down. In this regard, real physical abuse, or the danger of such, had to be directly confronted. For example, Ernest Ford recalls a time when he was "booted" by a passenger named Hayes. Ford explains that he received a good tip from Hayes's friends, who made the passenger feel very "harsh"; so in the end Ford made him look bad. Mr. Ford's story is not easy: he "accepts" the boot and rationalizes it. Sometimes you *had* to accept a boot. Sometimes you *could not*. This story is typical of a porter who is still working out in his own mind the line between being a servant and being a man.

Ernest Ford's story follows, and after it, a series of stories told (with one exception) by other porters. They are responses to that story, personal statements of each individual's feelings about the overall problem, and they are a communal statement of group norms. They depict the range of circumstances under which direct or indirect response—rationalization or confrontation—is called for. The discourse is marked by what William Labov refers to as an evaluative component, which he feels is characteristic of the performance of personal narratives. Richard Bauman describes the evaluative aspect of personal experience storytelling as an indicator of "the nature and intensity of the narrator's feelings concerning the experience he is recounting—why he considers it worth telling about."[50]

This entire exchange—in which Mr. Ford tells his story to several other porters, they react to it, and dialogue ensues—exemplifies the creative and experimental aspects, as well as the communally speculative and philosophical nature, of these storytelling sessions. With the stories and the storytelling sessions porters negotiate their own personal identities vis-à-vis the social identity of the group as a group. As Karmela Liebkind has suggested, a comparison of the self with a group will lead to a recognition of both similarities and differences.[51] The porters attempt to reconcile these in their narrative session. Narrative here is doing more than recapitulating experience and thus making it "real" by codifying and patterning it. It is a case of narrative having a creative function, of storytelling being an active agent in a contemporary social situation. It provides an axis for the group to negotiate and along which to define themselves.

Here is Ford's story about "booting":

> Well, Hayes was a big politician, it appeared, and he didn't like colored people. Ah, it was . . . and he was—he had an audience, and he just wanted to show some of his friends how they act down South, how they treat a nigger, you know. And so he gave me a boot, that's all, and I accepted it. And in the process of accepting it, his friends really didn't go along with him. And they were really with him for a while, then they said, "Well, we'll take care of it." So they took up a pot for me, and made my trip very pleasant. And they made him feel very harsh because they, if I recall right, they made him feel very below by making such an advance at a good porter, you know. And I didn't like it at all, and from then on I had a good trip because it was a special party, and Mr. Hayes thought he was being funny whereas he was really—he belittled himself by trying to belittle me.
>
> He missed the cuspidor and spit on the floor. Which I had to clean up, and I mentioned it to him that that's the reason those cuspidors was there, for him to spit in it. And he was going to show his friends how to treat a nigger, you know? And he booted me. I, of course, was in the process of cleaning it up at the time, and this is when his friends stopped playing cards with him and everything. They had a big game going on also, and they stopped playing the game and broke up the game and everything. But, of course, it was embarrassing, but ended up it was a very good trip.

Happy Davis:

> If that had been Talley, that wouldn't have happened. Talley would have been right on his head.

Ford:

Either you accept it or you reject it. It depends on what kind
of porter you are. Well, I accepted it, but of course I didn't
like it. But what can you do? If you tell the conductor, why,
he'll say, "Well, you know we have to get along," and so
forth.

Davis:

You could put it on there and hand it to the Pullman
conductor or the train conductor or the Pullman Company to
rectify that situation. You ain't supposed to get kicked out
there, man.

Another speaker:

I never had no experience like that, and I don't know how I
would have acted. That is the porter individual that reacts
to it and how he figured it out.

Ford:

I had a private party, and when you've got a private party,
you're trying to make some money. And everybody else was
being happy, and for one guy to be stupid, you just don't
ruin your whole trip by attacking this one party, because he
is part of the group. So you have to think fast, as to whether
you should accept this or reject it. And I accepted it because
there were witnesses saw that I had done no wrong to the
man, and of which he made my trip monetarily much
greater than it would have been had he not done this. And
he made himself miserable because they resented him doing
it. And they made it up.[52]

As Mr. Ford told his story, the other men listened with interest
and attention, but they registered shock, surprise, and disapproval
that Ford had, in his own words, "accepted" it. They cited another
man as an example of someone who would not have accepted it.
They offered alternatives: take it up with the company. "You ain't
supposed to get kicked out there, man," said Happy. Ernie, tem-
perature rising, explains in detail that by behaving as he did, he
won the sympathy of Hayes's companions. Had he behaved any
differently, he would have lost their sympathy and their tips as
well. As it was, the other passengers compensated Ford for the
indignity by taking up a collection and tipping him very generously.
"He belittled himself by trying to belittle me," he offers as justification for his actions.

The porters are discussing an instance of racism and abuse on the train that occurred long after the successful formation of the union. Ford is portraying himself in an instance of humiliation in which he attempts to save face by casting himself as the trickster who has the last laugh: he collects the money. This kind of passive aggression, silently suffering but collecting a tip, has been a common response to the imbalanced power structure the porters dealt with in a job where the customer was not only always right, he was also rich and white.

However, under the circumstances, it is not considered appropriate by the other porters, who are older than Mr. Ford and have seen firsthand worse conditions belonging to the days before the union's final successes. One man suggests taking advantage of the safeguards the union provided. The exchange continues as two other men tell of similar personal experiences. In these stories, one porter almost confronts the passenger but stops short of direct confrontation, rationalizing the situation instead. The other porter then tells a story in which the circumstances dictate that he take direct, confrontational action.

Homer Glenn:

> I went to New Orleans and I—on the way back after we left Lake Pontchartrain—I went to pick up two people in the back. And I came back through the club car with four bags, with two under each arm. One under each arm and one in each hand. And this man, he was pretty well loaded, sitting there with some woman, and he stopped me, put his foot up and says, "Say, don't you pull off your hat in the dining car?" I said, "I'm not in the dining car. If I was, I still wouldn't pull my hat off because I have no hand to hold it." He said, "Well, don't you come back through here with your hat on."
>
> Well, I was quite young then in the service, and I didn't care if I went up, and I told this old porter, I said, "I'm going back there. Give me my ice pick." So he told me, "It's not worth it." So, when I thought about it, well, there's a man that does not know what a dining car is from a club car, and if I go back there and create a problem, I'm just as stupid as he is. So I ignored the whole thing. I didn't go back there.[53]

L. C. Richie:

> Well, now, like Mr. Ford, I didn't have too much of that. I have had insults, yes, but I ignored them. Not every one,

no. Some I couldn't ignore. Some I had to challenge. I was in
Kansas City—or Arkansas—about sixteen or seventeen cars,
and we went down from a city down into the country, way
down to—I forget the name of the camp now—and of course
we picked up these soldiers, and that was during the time
that they were taking these soldiers, and taking them to
Atlantic City and putting them in hotels, so they could
airplane the group and so forth. Now, these boys were just
rednecks, crackers, as we called them, right out of the
bottom of the South. And of course, we went out there back
out in the country, and they loaded these guys on.
Everybody got on, two at a time. So, we were going to
Atlantic City. Now, we were leaving there, coming back up
to Arkansas to get on the main line, and during the time we
were coming back to get on the main line, I heard nothing
but "nigger." And to tell you the truth, I just didn't—well, I
didn't appreciate it. I ran regular for a long time and I ran in
the East quite a bit, and you didn't hear all of that. So, I
heard nothing but that all the time, coming back up to the
main line.

So, after we got on the main line we started off that
night, going out. And we had to stop at different stations, for
water and so forth, and these boys were using nothing but
"nigger." And they were sitting in the car saying, "Where'd
he go? Where'd he go? Where'd he go?" Well, I got out of
the way as much as I could and sat in the smoker. I sat in
the smoker, and I was saying to myself, "Should I jump out
of the window?" That's the truth. Because I just got filled up
to here. Finally I said, "I'm going out to the linen closet." I
went out to the linen closet, and the window jack was in the
linen closet. And as you all know, you can stand so they
can't see you in the aisle, and I took the window jack and
put it under my white coat. I got back out there and sat
down at the window. And just as I started down the hall,
back to the smoker, an apple hit the wall, right at the linen
closet. It hit that wall. *Throwing* it at me. Didn't intend to hit
me, I realized later, because they had let me go all the way
down the hall before they threw it.

I came back, I sat down for a second, and something just
hit me, and I came back, and I stood in the car, and I took
the window jack out and I said, "Goddamn you, every son of
a bitch in here!" Everybody stopped, just that quick. I said,
"I'll take this window jack, I'll—who threw that apple?" And

I walked down the aisle and said, "Goddamn you, everyone of you, get up!" Everyone, not a damn one stood up. "And I better not hear that again." And that's the truth. And I do not curse like that.

I came back and sat down, and *nobody*, nobody on my car after that used the word nigger. And all the other porters that were on those cars, they came up and rode in my car the rest of the night, because they heard what I did, and every car was using that word, and when we got to Atlantic City, every one of those sons o'bitches wouldn't open their mouth. Just as quiet as they can be.[54]

Taken together in sequence, as they were told, the stories present a range of responses to a particular kind of recurrent situation, and the appropriateness of those responses is hotly debated. Confrontation is considered inappropriate unless under circumstances of extreme provocation, while passive acceptance and rationalization is likewise appropriate only under certain circumstances. The porters find Mr. Ford's choice of passive acceptance, at best, debatable under the circumstances described. Most porters pride themselves on being able to avoid such situations, and, in fact, part of the skill of the job lies in being able to deflate potential crises before they have a chance to occur. Personal opinions are being expressed, as is personal identity, and it is through the collective expression of personal experience and personal identity that group norms are negotiated.

The tensions that arise from the servant-man dichotomy are found in other service positions also. Female airline flight attendants tell stories of smiling sweetly at an arrogant passenger until he carries his liberties too far. At this point of excessive transgression, defined differently by each flight attendant, her pride as a person overwhelms her desire for job security and her need to behave as a servant.[55] Unlike porters, however, who had a socially defined and shared category of identity based on gender to use as an alternative, female flight attendants have no culturally valued term "woman" that neatly counterparts the porters' "man." Mr. Richie's story during the exchange following the Hayes incident, on the other hand, tells how he was forced into a situation in which no response other than total rejection of the circumstances, and direct confrontation of them, would do. Any other response would be less than adequate and would not allow the porter to maintain the delicate balancing act of his position as a servant vis-à-vis his sense of himself as a man.

Although a porter is in control of the situation and functions as a host to the passenger, in order to perform and project the role of servant and protect his tip, he must not be seen to have the rights that are otherwise afforded to a host. Passengers are therefore allowed to take liberties with porters, and by doing so go out of their way to remind them of, and to reinforce, their subordinate status. These ideas are encapsulated, or named, in a Burkean sense, throughout porters' narratives.[56] In the dialogue cited previously (the recounting of the Hayes incident and the stories that follow) there is a chain association, and a degree of what Potter and Watson call "matching," that is, of saying, "I, too, experienced that sort of thing," but there is also a degree of differentiation, "I handled it slightly differently, and here's why."[57] The degree of differentiation is not polarization, which under the rules of these kinds of speech events would be considered aggressive and insulting, and therefore inappropriate. (Porters, always gentlemen, take great care not to really offend each other, although they jokingly insult each other frequently.) It is instead a gradual movement, a discussion of a range of alternatives. The conversation moves from an instance of acceptance of physical abuse, accompanied by a defense of that acceptance based on contextual factors, to an instance of confrontation of abusive passengers, also accompanied by a suggestion that the porter really had no other choice, and, significantly, nothing to lose. In between these two narratives we see instances of near-confrontation accompanied by descriptions of the circumstances that determined the porter's choice of response. Both individual identity and group concerns are being played out here: the narratives are simultaneously an expression of group homogeneity and personal identity. The narratives and the sequence in which they are told are artfully structured in such a way as to provide a generally meaningful symbolic statement about the categories of the porters' lives and the range of possibilities available to them within those categories.

The central concern addressed is of being perceived as buyable, as property. In the cycle of narratives recounted in the previous chapter about A. Philip Randolph and the blank check, we see Randolph exhibit the ultimate control over the corrupting influences of the white world. This theme permeates porters' lore: they tell stories of individuals who resist taking money left out as a test, and they tell stories of porters who bribe dispatchers for preferred runs. They disparage these men as the real Uncle Toms, because they have adopted the corrupt system wherein men can be bought and sold. They recall other tipping humiliations, great and small, and they are almost universally familiar with the blank check story. As the Pullman Company attempted to buy Randolph, so did the white world buy and sell black people, and white passengers attempt to buy black porters. The connections are direct; that is why, in one of the versions of the blank check story, Randolph is reported to have referred to slavery by saying, "You could buy my parents, but you can't buy me." He, and all Negroes, are "not for sale."

The A. Philip Randolph blank check stories, although told conversationally, were not told in the *same* conversation. Those stories ranged from total rejection of the check, to pretended acceptance, to at least one story of pretended rejection but actual acceptance of the check. Since the stories are told by individuals, this variation is related to the individual teller's needs and other personal variables, although the stories are important to porters in general. If we view the sequence of narratives that is comprised of the Hayes anecdote and the discourse that followed about dealing with abusive passengers, we see that each narrative, addressing the same general topic, offers a change, or transformation in the actions described, as well as suggesting different strategies for each set of variables defined. Together, they can be seen as a series of narratives ranging from one alternative pole to the other. On the topic of abuse, then, the narratives feature behavior ranging from total acceptance to total confrontation. The contexts of the events are determining variables: porters recognize that one only rebels or confronts under extreme provocation, and likewise, acceptance is appropriate only when there is no other alternative. It is the consideration of the variables that determines the proper strategies. Either of the two polar positions, if adopted without the legitimizing circumstances, is criticized.

In the case of the stories of A. Philip Randolph and the blank check, the stories can also be seen to range from one pole to the other, from acceptance (of the check) to rejection. So the range that is present in a single conversation (the Hayes dicussion) is also present in a group of stories of many different conversations about the same subject. Examining the narratives throughout this book, we find stories featuring responses ranging from acceptance to rejection around any one issue. The gradual range from complete acceptance to complete rejection of passenger abuse is mirrored inversely in the blank check stories on the subject of being bought. However, since the abuse issue is directly tied to the tipping issue, the stories are related to each other. The conversation about Hayes has different men in different circumstances doing gradually different things, while the Randolph stories have the same man, in the same circumstances, doing gradually different things: he dramatically rejects the check with a flourish; or he pretends to accept it, but rejects it; or he keeps it, but never cashes it; or he fills it in to an uncashable amount; or he accepts it, but pretends to reject it. These are legends of a heroic model, and they parallel stories about porters accepting "booting," which range from the porter who accepts a kick but takes a tip to a porter who would not have let it happen, from advice to report it to a story of a porter who almost confronts a passenger but finally rationalizes the situation ("Here's a man who don't know a club car from a dining car"), to a story of a porter who did confront the passengers.

Each set of stories deals with similar ideas. The blank check stories deal with bribery and the idea of men as buyable, as property. The passenger stories deal with the immediate concern of abuse, but also with the larger idea of being treated as property. The dualities of servant versus man, and of high and low status, are foregrounded and negotiated in these stories and in others like them. Moreover, one can see this conversation as the recapitulation of a long historical process of dealing directly, through unionization, and indirectly, through narrative, with the same or similar problems. Just as the abuse issue can be seen as a transformation of the tipping issue, so are these historical episodes and narratives transformations of each other. In that sense, we are dealing with transformations of transformations. The emotion is heightened in such conversations, as they are, in fact, episodes in an ongoing debate as to the parameters of acceptable behavior for porters, along this axis of servant-man.

Storytelling among porters is a performance genre marked with great oratorical skill and flourish. It is also a fictive arena for exploring possible responses and the circumstances under which those responses are appropriate. By establishing a set of rules that relate certain circumstances to certain behaviors, the porters are able to position themselves along the continuum and understand or explain their own particular responses. The contradictions they faced were, and still are, deeply disturbing. The group creation of the terms of this continuum aids the porters in justifying their own actions. The storytelling is both a presentation of personal identity and an arena in which personal identity is negotiated by the group.[58] Both personal and cultural perspectives are provided. It becomes a communal discourse, almost philosophical, on the right way to behave. By discussing these issues, the porters come to reconcile the contradictions and to understand better their universe, the world they lived in, the world they were contained by.

For the record, ice picks were a standard part of a train's equipment and a tool which a porter used often. When, in the testimony above, Homer Glenn first decides to confront a passenger, it is going to be with an ice pick in his hand. The fact that he was cooled down by an older porter does not alter the gravity of the situation. Mr. Glenn is a quiet, eloquent, and gentle man; it is most disconcerting to hear him speak of such ugly thoughts. However, porters did have to confront passengers, as Mr. Richie demonstrated with his story. Other porters did, too, as they tell in other stories. Hunter Johnson also passed rough words with a passenger and threatened him with the ice pick he carried. He, too, locates his actions in a context in which confrontation was important for his own personal sense of dignity. He goes on to mention a porter who actually stabbed this same passenger with a knife. This is the most extreme incident we have so far encountered, and it should be seen in the context of the continuum mentioned earlier. These are extreme reactions to extreme provocations, as defined by individual porters.

Hunter Johnson discusses the problem:

> There are ways to cool a man down. I brought a man from
> St. Louis, and he got kind of violent at night. He went into
> his bedroom, and he carried his girl in there with him. And
> I knew she was in there, so I went and got the conductor
> and told him about it. He came and knocked *and* knocked
> *and* knocked. He wouldn't even answer. Great big son of a
> gun. And what got me, I made his bed down, and she got in
> the bed and messed the bed up. So finally, they got him out
> of there, and he was sleeping in my car. He said, "Did you
> get the conductor, Pullman?" "Me?" I said. "No, I didn't get
> him." He said, "If I thought so, I'd kick your so-and-so." I
> said, "No, you wouldn't. You wouldn't do that to *me*.
> Because there's a way to stop you." I carried an ice pick
> down in the holes of my belt all the time to chop up ice. I
> said, "You ain't going to do that to me. You might do it to
> other people, but you ain't going to do it to me and get away
> with it." So he went on about his business. And on his way
> back to St. Louis, he slapped a porter right here in
> Baltimore, that same man. And this porter almost cut him to
> death if someone didn't hold him down. I know the porter.
> He would have cut him to death. I didn't carry no knife. I
> carried an ice pick in my holes all the time. But I didn't go
> out there for no violence. I didn't go for that.[59]

The servant-man dichotomy was paralleled in the larger society by the stereotypes of the porters in the popular media, which exaggerated the servile aspects of the job, as compared to the realities of the men and their occupation. The following chapter will examine these stereotypes and compare them with the porters' self-images as encapsulated in their narratives. Before moving on to that, however, a final word on the servant-man issue. Homer Glenn, who suggested these terms in his own words, reflected on the fact that porters had to reconcile the two roles. They were not necessarily contradictory, he explained when asked.

> I think you *can*. I think you can be a man while being a servant. I think if you have the courage and dignity and respect for yourself, and respect for people, that you can be a man while being a servant.[60]

In their own ways, other porters concur. William Harrington says:

> You were a servant. That was my job. And the better service you gave, the more would come your way in tips. You were a servant. You *served* the people. I *served* my people and was glad to serve them. And I gave them the *best* service that I *could* give them. And that's what people appreciate today, and that's what I appreciate.[61]

Hunter Johnson asserts:

> You could be both. You could be a servant and a man. You didn't steal nothing from them. That was the man part. You didn't try to mess with any of the women on the train. You had spotters out there.
>
> None of them ever tried me, because I kept myself in a way, I guess. They'd try me, I would have cussed them out. I don't care *who* it was.
>
> I promised my instructor, Jim Thompson, I would be a man. I was a man. Until my last trip I never did get into no trouble.
>
> So, it was a strange experience for me. I wouldn't want to do it *over* again. I wished I'd come out from the railroad company during the war and got me a government job. Because you could work yourself up in the government. You couldn't work no higher than a porter-in-charge. But I'm happy. I draw enough to live on, my little house here's been paid for. And I'm happy.[62]

Being a servant was a role the porters played. They put it on and took it off along with that white jacket they once admired from afar. Despite the problems, they maintained their dignity. To give service was a job, a skill, even an art. They vigorously resisted the tendency to internalize the role, with its attendant stereotypes, and confuse it with their personal identities, their self-worth. Giving service well—doing your job well—did not make you an Uncle Tom. Betraying your dignity, betraying a fellow porter, allowing yourself to be bought by the system: these actions killed community and fraternity. These were the actions of an Uncle Tom. The porters' struggle to resist corrupting influences is a heroic one, and their stories, of A. Philip Randolph, and of their own daily trials, encapsulate it.

NOTES

1. See, for instance, Raymond Williams, *The Sociology of Culture* (New York: Schocken Books, 1982).

2. Barry Lee Pearson, *"Sounds So Good to Me": The Bluesman's Story* (Philadelphia: University of Pennsylvania Press, 1984).

3. See, for instance, Norm Cohen, *Long Steel Rail: The Railroad in American Folksong* (Urbana: University.of Illinois Press, 1981). Other important recent studies of the blues include David Evans, *Big Road Blues: Tradition and Creativity in Folk Blues* (Berkeley: University of California Press, 1982); William Ferris, *Blues from the Delta* (Garden City, N.Y.: Anchor Books, 1979); and Robert Palmer, *Deep Blues* (New York: The Viking Press, 1981).

4. Ernest Ford, Jr., July 2, 1987.

5. Leon Long, July 17, 1982.

6. Pamela Bradney, "The Joking Relationship in Industry," *Human Relations* 10 (1957): 179–87.

7. Ernest Ford, Jr., May 1, 1978.

8. Lawrence W. Davis, July 7, 1984.

9. See Roger D. Abrahams, *Afro-American Folktales* (New York: Pantheon Books, 1985) 14, 263–95; Richard M. Dorson, *American Negro Folktales* (Greenwich, Conn.: Fawcett Books, 1968); and Lawrence W. Levine, *Black Culture and Black Consciousness: Afro-American Folk Thought from Slavery to Freedom* (New York: Oxford University Press, 1977), 121–35. For some published slave narratives collected by the Works Progress Administration, see Eugene D. Genovese, *Roll, Jordan, Roll: The World the Slaves Made* (New York: Random House, 1974).

10. Lawrence W. Davis, July 7, 1984.

11. Lawrence W. Davis, July 1, 1978.

12. Leroy Shackleford, May 16, 1980.

13. William Harrington, July 16, 1982.

14. Lawrence W. Davis, July 1, 1984.

15. William Harrington, July 16, 1982.

16. Leon Long, July 7, 1982.

17. See, for example, Richard M. Dorson, *America in Legend* (New York: Pantheon Press, 1973), 57–79.

18. C. L. Dellums, November 13, 1980.

19. Lawrence W. Davis, May 5, 1980.

20. Fred Fair, March 30, 1983.

21. Homer Glenn, August 18, 1980.

22. Walter Cole, October 8, 1983.

23. Clarence J. Talley, May 3, 1978.

24. Erving Goffman, *The Presentation of Self in Everyday Life* (Garden City, N.Y.: Doubleday Anchor Books, 1959), 106–40; Edward M. Swift and Charles S. Boyd, "A Pullman Porter Looks at Life," *Psychoanalytic Review* 15 (1928): 393–496; Bernard Mergen, "The Pullman Porter: From 'George' to Brotherhood," *The South Atlantic Quarterly* 75 (1974): 225.

25. Ernest Ford, Jr., November 14, 1980.

26. Mergen, 225.

27. Rex Stewart, May 17, 1980.

28. Leon Long, July 7, 1982.

29. Leroy C. Richie, May 8, 1978.

30. See Victor Turner, "Betwixt and Between: The Liminal Period in *Rites de Passage*," in Victor Turner, *The Forest of Symbols: Aspects of Ndembu Ritual* (Ithaca, N.Y.: Cornell University Press, 1970), 93–111. See also Arnold van Gennep, *The Rites of Passage* (Chicago: University of Chicago Press, 1960).

31. Homer Glenn, November 14, 1980.

32. Ibid.

33. Leroy C. Richie, July 7, 1984.

34. Leroy C. Richie, November 4, 1982.

35. Leon Long, July 7, 1982.

36. Leroy C. Richie, April 7, 1980.

37. Lawrence W. Davis, February 7, 1983.

38. Hunter Johnson, July 12, 1983.

39. Harris, 199.

40. William Harrington, July 16, 1982.

41. Green Glenn, April 1987.

42. William D. Miller, May 6, 1978. Roger Abrahams has suggested that this narrative may be a version of an international tale-type. See his " 'The House Burned Down' Again," *Journal of American Folklore* 76: 337–39.

43. Brotherhood of Sleeping Car Porters, *The Pullman Porter, the Benefits of His Racial Monopoly*, no author listed, no date.

44. A. Philip Randolph, *Freemen Yet Slaves Under "Abe" Lincoln's Son*, (Chicago: Brotherhood of Sleeping Car Porters, 1926).

45. Marisa Zavalloni, "Ego-ecology: The Study of the Interaction between Social and Personal Identities," in Anita Jacobson-Widding, ed., *Identity: Personal and Socio-Cultural*.

46. Samuel Beasley, August 18, 1980.

47. Fred Fair, March 30, 1983.

48. Hunter Johnson, July 12, 1983.

49. Homer Glenn, November 18, 1980.

50. Richard Bauman, *Verbal Art as Performance* (Prospect Heights, Ill.: Waveland Press, Inc., 1984), 26; William Labov, *Language in the Inner City* (Philadelphia: University of Pennsylvania Press, 1972), 354–96.

51. Karmela Liebkind, "Dimensions of Identity in Multiple Group Allegiance: Reconstruction through Intergroup Identification," in Anita Jacobson-Widding, ed., *Identity*, 188.

52. Lawrence W. Davis, Ernest Ford, Jr., and L. C. Richie, November 14, 1980.

53. Homer Glenn, November 14, 1980.

54. Leroy C. Richie, November 14, 1980.

55. Jack Santino, " 'Flew the Ocean in a Plane': An Investigation of Airline Occupational Narrative," *Journal of the Folklore Institute* 15 (1978): 189–208.

56. See, for example, Kenneth Burke, *A Rhetoric of Motives* (Berkeley: University of California Press, 1969), and "Literature as Equipment for Living," in Burke, *The Philosophy of Literary Form: Studies in Symbolic Action* (Berkeley: University of California Press, 1973).

57. Jeanne Watson and Robert J. Potter, "An Analytic Unit for the Study of Interaction," *Human Relations* 15 (1962): 245–63.

58. Watson and Potter, 246; see also Richard Bauman, "The LaHave Island General Store: Sociability and Verbal Art in a Nova Scotia Community," *Journal of American Folklore* 85 (1972): 330–43; and Jack Santino, "Miles of Smiles, Years of Struggle: The Negotiation of Black Occupational Identity through Personal Experience Narrative," *Journal of American Folklore* 96 (1983): 393–412.

59. Hunter Johnson, July 12, 1983.

60. Homer Glenn, November 14, 1980.

61. William Harrington, July 16, 1982.

62. Hunter Johnson, July 12, 1983.

5. Popular Images and Stereotypes

> The porter has often been depicted as an object of ridicule in movies and songs. He had to struggle against this popular image of himself as an Uncle Tom.
>
> —Mrs. Rosina Tucker

One of the great ironies in the lives of Pullman porters is that even though they broke through barriers of race prejudice to overcome the resistance of years of entrenched dogma, and challenged the might of the industrial giant, the Pullman Company, to form an unprecedented black labor union, they were served up to the public by the popular media in images of grinning, obsequious, scheming Uncle Toms.

A stereotype is a generalization based upon one or a few characteristics, often exaggerated, which carries with it an implied value judgment, usually negative. Sometimes it is argued that there can be good stereotypes, such as the image of American Indians as "noble savages," for instance, but since even supposedly positive images do not accurately describe the people they refer to, nor realistically reflect reality, stereotypes are ultimately always harmful. Pullman porters were stereotyped in a negative way in American culture generally, by the Pullman Company itself, and also in the popular media. Such stereotypification can certainly be said to have benefited the Pullman Company. Since it was selling service to the public, the company needed to create the perception that its service workers were many things: trustworthy, to be sure, but never threatening. Loyal, docile, childlike, happy in their work—these were the qualities the company wished to project regarding its porters. The fact that the service positions were filled by black men was in itself a major reinforcement of a social stereotype that had its roots in slavery and in the plantation mentality the company maintained. A Negro servant working a luxurious vehicle of transportation was presented as part of the natural order of things. Passengers might behave kindly toward porters, or even engage in intimate conversation with them, but at no time were porters considered anything but inferior by virtue of their race, reinforced by their subordinate job roles. Racism, the belief in inherent physiological, emotional, and intellectual differences and inequalities among races, underpinned the rationalization for keeping porters in their place.

In its publicity photos, the Pullman Company showed the public a kindly, avuncular porter. These images were directed at travelers who may have wondered at some time or other if these men ever resented their menial status. The figures in the publicity shots reassured passengers. They created misleading images of happy, simple men who got no greater pleasure in life than waiting on rich white people, and who wanted only a pat on the head and perhaps a shiny quarter for their efforts. These stereotypes were reinforced by images of porters in popular songs and motion pictures. The first place to look for the basic stereotype, however, is in the Pullman Company publicity drawings and photos, because these feature the image of the porter that the company itself wished to project.

The Pullman Company shots, used for advertising purposes, depicted the porter in three basic situations: with adult passengers, taking care of children, or working by himself. He is at all times contented, happy, even appreciative of his lot and his position. Still, he is a bit of a buffoon as he stifles a giggle while looking into the camera, and shares with the viewer—us—the joke that the passenger is holding his magazine upside-down. There is nothing inherently offensive in this picture, but if it is compared to a candid shot of a porter talking to a little girl, the contrast is stark. The candid photo shows us a warm, gentle soul, genuinely affectionate toward his young charge. The Pullman photo gives us a clown.

Any such comparison of staged publicity photos with candid shots of porters reveals this dichotomy. Given the nature of the job and the industry, it is to be expected. More interesting are the stylized drawn renditions of porters in the company's advertising campaigns. These show us porters with the facial features of Caucasians. Only their shaded skin says they are black, and the shading here is lightly done. The drawings tell the Pullman customers that it is safe to entrust their children to these men because they are almost white.

Drawing lends itself to caricature. That is, it is easier to draw a stereotype than it is to photograph one. Jeff Todd Titon has noted this phenomenon in his study of blues recording advertisements of the same general era, in that the often-outlandish or at least unusual situations described in the songs were able to be depicted on the record sleeves in drawings rather than any other medium.[1] Indeed, there was a standard, formulaic, graphic rendering of Negroes according to racist stereotypes, and the popular images of Pullman porters conform to it in certain ways, but differ significantly in others. The drawing of a porter running anxiously to submit a suggestion shows us a subordinate who is eager to please and happy with his circumstances, but the gross exaggeration of physical features found on the record sleeves of the 1920s is not present. Ironically, in this situation the company was caught in the same kind of paradox the porters were. On the one hand, it needed a subservient class of workers, laborers who accepted lower pay for work equal to that of a conductor, because they had no choice. On the other hand, those workers, although perceived as inferior by passengers, must also, in their way, be as elegant as the cars they rode and the passengers they served. They must contribute to the overall genteel ambience of the rail travel experience that the company needed to create, otherwise the white clientele might shy away. Of course, the concept of well-heeled Negro servants was well established. The men hired to work as porters were chosen to conform to this image. Thus, they were highly qualified, often overqualified men, noticeably dignified and intelligent. The racism that kept these men from going further professionally also helped create the work force to populate the position of dignified, trustworthy servant. In a triple twist, this same racism painted the majority of blacks as untrustworthy and possibly dangerous. The company had to ensure that it was the former rather than the latter stereotype that was promulgated. The figures in the company's drawings and publicity releases amounted to a kind of propaganda that portrayed porters as dignified but willingly, and even eagerly, subservient.

Rather than exaggerate Negro features, as was done on the record sleeve drawings of the period, the portrayals in the Pullman drawings are *devoid* of characteristically Negro features. Nevertheless, the drawings communicate the quality of an inferior anxiously trying to please his superiors, not simply a man trying to do his job well. It is important to note that the more condescending and demeaning graphic renditions were intended for the porters themselves; the renditions of porters with essentially white features were aimed at the general public. The company was making two very different statements. With the one kind of depiction it was telling porters that they were dumb and in need of paternal (corporate) guidance. With the others it was telling the traveling public to have no fear, to place their trust in these men who were just like them except for their dark skin, which placed them as servants.

Cartoons caricature these black working men as silly, dumb, confused, and dependent. They showed porters as childish—cute and well meaning, perhaps, but in need of guidance. Motion pictures also drew broad caricatures of Pullman porters. *The Girl on the Pullman,* for instance, a silent movie released in 1927, is a comedy of errors in which a man somehow marries twice. He rides the same Pullman car with his second bride as he did with his first. The Pullman porter, portrayed by a white actor in blackface, blackmails him for a tip. "Don't you remember me, boss? I was your porter on the honeymoon you took just before this one." As the porter leers at him greedily, the embarrassed passenger slips him a coin. Bowing and grinning, the porter exits from the berth. Outside the compartment, he bites the coin. Delighted to confirm that it is the real thing, he flips the coin into the air and clicks his heels as he savors his triumph.[2]

As we have seen in the porters' folklore that we have examined earlier, tips were of major economic importance to porters. Therefore, like the shining of shoes, getting tips became associated with porters. A preoccupation with tips became one of the stereotypical attributes of the standard popular image. In *Long Steel Rail,* author Norm Cohen says that in one minstrel song fragment, the treatment of baggage by black railroad porters was viewed with some suspicion.[3] He quotes the following verse which encapsulates the attitude that because porters performed their labor with the intention of receiving recompense, they were not to be trusted:

> We're jolly rail-road porters
> And we push for jobs with spunk,
> Bekase we fill our vittal chests
> By gettin' people's trunks.[4]

In another snippet of song, the theme of the rural black man who aspires to be a Pullman porter rather than work menial labor is touched upon. Rather than see this desire as a positive attempt on the part of black men to improve their situations, it is portrayed as uppity:

> The Alabama Niggers
> They think they are mighty smart.
> They'd rather work a railroad
> Than drive a hoss and cart.[5]

From a 1926 volume by Odum and Johnson, *Negro Workaday Songs*, comes this "Negro minstrel type" called "Pullman Porter." The inconsistencies in capitalizing Pullman are in the song text as printed in that volume.

Runs from California
Plumb up to Maine.
I's a Negro porter
On de pullman train.
Pullman train,
Pullman train,
I's de Negro porter
On de pullman train.

Braid on the cap an'
Buttons in a row,
On that blue uniform
Right down the fo'
In pullman train,
Pullman train,
I's a Negro porter
On de pullman train.

It's a tip right here
And a tip right thar,
Tip all along
Up an' down the pullman car.
Pullman train,
Pullman train,
I's a Negro porter
On de pullman train.

Pocket full o' money,
Stomach full o' feed,
What next in the worl'
Do a fellow need?
Pullman train,
Pullman train,
I's a Negro porter
On de Pullman train.[6]

Notice that in this song, porters are said to have a pocket full of money and a stomach full of feed. They are shown to be well-off and happy-go-lucky. The reality these songs describe is accurate only insofar as porters performed with tips in mind, as they must, and were proud of their uniforms. The representation of these ideas is done in a demeaning pseudo-dialect that was standard fare of the era. Ironically, where porters' stories emphasize the porters' honesty, the popular songs of white people speak of distrust.

In films, the porter was usually portrayed as a fool. The 1906 movie, *The Hold-Up of the Rocky Mountain Express*, for example, plays on the porter-as-buffoon image. The porter is shown stumbling and falling while carrying a full tray, simultaneously being attacked by an indignant woman who hits him repeatedly with her umbrella. He pleases nobody. The film is cruel: it portrays the porter as dazed and confused, overwhelmed by the amount and complexity of his work. The audience is made to laugh at him. He is helpless; he has no control over the events or the situation. The audience is made to scorn him rather than sympathize with his plight. Once again, the public image is precisely the opposite of the occupational reality: the porters were very much in control of their cars and their passengers; they negotiated for control with conductors (rather than caving in to their authority or seeking parental guidance from them); and eventually, through the union, they gained some control over other problem areas as well. The film actually demonstrates just how demanding a porter's job was; unfortunately, it does that without sensitivity or sympathy. Perhaps it was because porters really had such control that white people needed reassurance that they were innocuous and foolish.[7]

The same can be said of a popular recording of 1923 by Collins and Harlan which is sung in the first person: "We needs no introduction, you can see just who we are, porters on a Pullman train." The song becomes a small drama as passengers are heard calling to the porter:

> Porter, come here, sir,
> Porter, stay there,
> Porter, the pillow is as hard as a rock,
> Porter, please give me more air.
> Porter, come here, sir,
> Porter, stay there.
> All night the people complain.
> We is porters, dandy porters,
> and we ride on the vestibule train.

The porters in the song, as in life, are

> Standing on the platform of the sleeping car
> Ready, quick, and willing to explain.

All they ask is a little friendly tip:

> We think you oughtta
> Give us a quarter
> And then you'll have a very pleasant trip.

The well-known song, "Shuffle Off to Buffalo," from the *Broadway Limited* film, uses the same rhyme: "For a little silver quarter we can have the Pullman porter turn the lights down low." Here, the reference to the porter is for verisimilitude, simply as a detail of the setting. In Collins and Harlan's "Porters on a Pullman Train," however, like the film *The Girl on the Pullman*, the porter cares only for the tip. The implied blackmail of the song ("Give us a quarter and then you'll have a very pleasant trip") suggests the blackmail displayed by the porter on the screen. Purporting to present a porter's point of view, the song distorts the truth and gives credence to its opposite. While implicitly recognizing the power of the porter, the fact that he is in control, these images portray the porter as scheming and somewhat underhanded. This is a white response to a situation—black men in control—that is threatening.

This song also contains another aspect of the porters' popular image, the porter as dandy:

> There's something about a darkie
> Dressed in Pullman Blue.

The same image is contained in the song "Pullman Porters on Parade." In fact, the entire song is a paean to the idea that Pullman porters were dandies. Probably because of their real dignity, their higher wages relative to other black workers, and their cosmopolitanism due to being well traveled, porters were reduced to fops in the white media. Again an essential truth, in this case the dignity and care with which they carried themselves, was reduced to an exaggerated and ridiculous caricature. As a fop, the cosmopolitan porter was no longer threatening; he was back to being a joke. A second stereotype was being drawn upon, that of the stylish, urbane black man who was threatening to whites because he was not a country bumpkin.

Not every film or every song played on these stereotypes, but the exceptions were rare. One such exception has been mentioned earlier, *The Emperor Jones*, a film based on the play by Eugene O'Neill. This motion picture presented an accurate portrait of a porter's life and work. The porter, played by Paul Robeson, is shown leaving his family and friends in a small American town. Unlike the minstrel show excerpts previously discussed, this movie accurately describes the status of the porter among members of his home community, his work skills, and the occupational camaraderie of the job.[8]

A view from the other side is provided by Johnny Cash, who sang as his first release on the legendary Sun Record label in Memphis, Tennessee, a song he wrote called "Hey, Porter." The song paints a picture of a young man returning home from the army, anxiously asking the porter, "Hey, porter, is this train on time?" Servicemen did ride Pullman cars, and as in "Shuffle Off to Buffalo," the porter is used as a realistic detail upon which to hang a song. Cash represents in the song his own experience as a white country boy who rides the railroad home from a stint in the armed services, innocently and routinely requesting help from the porter. The porter himself bridges the worlds of black and white in his role as servant to those who rode the Pullman cars, and as such, was an important mediator of culture.

Porters are well represented in literature. In recent novels such as Alex Haley's *Roots*, the job is shown to be a rung on the ladder to social advancement for a black family.[9] In James MacPherson's *Hue and Cry*, the porter's life and work are sensitively described.[10] Both authors are black men, and both indicate that it is possible today to look back on the role porters played in society and appreciate their problems and contributions. Older works did not assess the porter in any historical or social context; rather, they used stereotypes of porters in a kind of literary shorthand, relying on the public's understanding of what the stereotype stood for. The porter was often used as a comic figure, and instead of developing characterization, authors let the almost cartoon-like caricature do the work for them. The popular 1924 picaresque novel, *Epic Peters, Pullman Porter*, features a porter as a fool who unwittingly does the right thing and unintentionally saves the day. This work of fiction contains a great many demeaning passages, especially as regards tipping. For example: "He thrust a dollar bill into the unreluctant hand of Mr. Peters. That colored gentleman bowed profusely." Also mentioned is the "not unwilling hand of the gangling porter." However, these descriptions are balanced by passages wherein the porter is not performing for the public ("bowing profusely") but instead taking pride in his work: "Epic closed the vestibule of his car and strolled inside. All twelve sections were made down and he gazed the length of green curtained canon, experiencing anew the thrill which had been his on the occasion of his maiden run."[11] The author, Octavus Roy Cohen, seems to be aware of the public-private dichotomy that porters faced. They had to be subservient to passengers, but the fact was they were working men who took pride in their cars and their work.

Epic Peters is portrayed in the book in the familiar childlike, dependent fashion when he is in the presence of white authority figures, but in one episode in the book he is shown more realistically, constantly being asked to do certain tasks by two passengers who are at cross-purposes with each other. Peters does as he is asked, collecting tips along the way. The story is similar to narratives porters actually tell, such as the story W. D. Miller told earlier of the passenger whose daughter ran away to New York. The study of the real folklore of Pullman porters makes it possible to weed out the formulaic stereotypical descriptions from the realities of the occupation.

In general, novelists are much more sympathetic in their renditions of porters than are cartoonists, songwriters, or other more popular artists. The popular arts unfortunately too often validate culture as it is, rather than challenge it. Probably because of its commercial nature, creators working in the popular arts tend to fullfill the expectations of its audiences, rather than break them. Thus, in works of literature such as Sinclair Lewis's famed novel *Babbit*, the author depicts a Pullman passenger who is guilty of all the hypocritical biases we have seen in this book, but does so in an ironic way. Lewis's irony is intentional, and is particularly effective seen in the context of the porters' true life experiences. Lewis portrays the routine racism porters faced masquerading as concern and even patriotism. He describes the perception that Negroes who attempt to better themselves are overextending themselves and upsetting the natural order of things. The porter is in a no-win situation in Lewis's fictional scene: Babbit erroneously assures his traveling mate that the train is running late. When a porter enters the car and is asked if the train is late, the porter contradicts Babbit and says the train is on time. Having answered a passenger simply, politely, and truthfully, the porter finds his conduct interpreted as "uppity." Following below is the scene:

"What time do we get into Pittsburg?" asked Babbit.

"Pittsburg? I think we get in at—no, that was last year's schedule—wait a minute—let's see—got a time-table right here."

"I wonder if we're on time?"

"Yuh, sure, we must be just about on time."

"No, we aren't—we were seven minutes late, last station."

"Were we? Straight? Why, gosh, I thought we were right on time."

"No, we're about seven minutes late."

"Yuh, that's right, seven minutes late."

The porter entered—a negro in white jacket with brass buttons.

"How late are we, George?" growled the fat man.

"Deed, I don't know, sir. I think we're about on time," said the porter, folding towels and deftly tossing them up on the rack above the washbowls. The council stared at him gloomily and when he was gone they wailed:

"I don't know what's come over these niggers, nowadays. They never give you a civil answer."

"That's a fact. They're getting so they don't have a single bit of respect for you. The old-fashioned coon was a fine old cuss—knew his place—but these young dinges don't want to be porters or cotton-pickers. Oh, no! They got to be lawyers and professors and Lord knows what all! I tell you, it's becoming a pretty serious problem. We ought to get together and show the black man, yes, and the yellow man, his place. Now, I haven't got one particle of race-prejudice. I'm the first to be glad when a nigger succeeds—so long as he stays where he belongs and doesn't try to usurp the rightful authority and business ability of the white man."[12]

Just as porters' stories about getting tips were compared earlier to the superficial approach to the subject as depicted in song, it is instructive to compare the porters' own words and stories with these photographs, film descriptions, and popular songs. Although Sinclair Lewis was deliberately satirical in Babbit, and The Emperor Jones was an honest and accurate film, for the most part porters were shown as types, not individuals, as inferior and perhaps a bit bothersome, only to be tolerated because of their enthusiasm and eagerness to please, and, of course, for the service they provided. When compared to the real stories porters tell, the reference to tipping in the old minstrel song is illuminated by our collection of tales on the subject. The touching testimony in the first chapter about leaving home, leaving overalls behind, is in sharp contrast to the "uppity" stereotype of those men who do not want to work a "hoss and cart" forever. The image, generally, is of a crafty yet bumbling, conniving but childish, greedy but stupid man. But once again, we find that porters themselves tell a different story, or more accurately, a series of stories. They tell of times they saved lives or performed acts of heroism, of charity, and even love for their passengers. The men feel that it is very important that an alternative image of porters be entered into the record; these narratives in some part counter the kinds of negative stereotypes seen above and were developed in response to them.

Hunter Johnson says, for instance:

> I was a hero once. A young woman got on the train out in Indiana, with a young baby, five days old. And she was nothing but a stranger in size. And she was going up in New Jersey to see her husband before he shipped out. And they got iron steps. And so she was walking about three steps behind me—I got her little bag—her heel caught and she was falling over that young baby. She would have killed that baby and probably hurt herself badly, too. And I dropped the bags and turned around and grabbed her and jumped four or five steps with her in my arms. So, I put her on another train, and when I came back a white fella shook my hand and said, "Porter, you know, you're a hero. She might have sent you a fortune." I said, "No, all I want to do is save that baby." I was shaking all over. She fell five or six steps with a young baby. That's the worst thing that ever happened to me on the road, and the best thing, because I saved a life, I believe, that morning.[13]

Rex Stewart:

> There's a lot of people in Wisconsin that rode these trains. Rex they will remember. I used to pass through the train, during the Depression, I'd see people on their way up to the country sitting up in the coach, former sleeping car people. "Oh, hello, Rex, glad to see you. How are you?" I'd say, "What are you doing sitting up here? Go on back, get in bed, get a good night's rest." Now, the Pullman Company never knew this.
>
> I served many of them because they served me, because they were good to me. I didn't forget them in their hour of depression. Many of them lost everything they had.[14]

How could such men be considered buffoons? The epithet "George," by which they were known generically, did much to create and maintain the stereotypes. As we have seen, the term was associated with the days of slavery, because it identified porters as the property of George Pullman, with all the associated ramifications of inferiority and childlike dependency. As such, A. Philip

Randolph insisted there be porters' name cards in each Pullman car, and he recognized that this symbolic change altering the term of address was as important as the more tangible improvements that increased pay and lessened hours. "George" is in many ways the sum total of the stereotype, and porters tried their best to ignore it, as in the following story by A. C. Speight. In this account, Porter Speight uses the term "ig" for ignore, when he refers to the practice of pretending not to hear the offending passenger:

> Yes, they'd call you George, all right. This is when they begun to, I don't remember what year it was now, but they begun to put your name—you had a name card. The name card, it was put on the end of the car. "This car is being served by porter so-and-so." They gave you a name. We didn't have the name, like, on your uniforms. No, you didn't have one on your uniform, only at the end of the car. If a passenger called you George, mostly sometimes, you would just ignore them because you know your name's not George, so therefore, just pass on by. That's the reason I say, coming out of Texas, the man, he called me "nigger." His wife says, "Don't say that." He said, "He's a nigger, ain't he?" I didn't say nothing, just kept on going, just igged him, that's all. Some things it's better off not saying anything, because wherever you were, you'd get in trouble, see. You learned that as part of the game. Ig him. Just tell him, "Those are your words; they aren't mine." Just pay him no attention.[15]

On his very first trip out, Hunter Johnson was called "George," and in the story below, he describes how he confronted the passenger:

> I had one woman—one woman—and at that time we just had a meeting here at Washington, and we had name cards. Company told me, told all of us, if they call you out of your name, just get your card and show it to them, or tell them your name. The very first trip I made, I was serving scotch and soda to three women sitting over on one side of the lounge car. And this little schoolteacher gets on at Columbia, coming up to Raleigh, and I come through and she says, "Hey George, will you get me a Coca-Cola, please?" I didn't stop walking. I walked on into the car and got my name card and brought it back. I said, "Lady, this is my name." I said, "You can call me porter, or you can call me Johnson, but *George* is not on the train today!" I didn't get her the Coca-Cola, neither.[16]

It was not the service aspect of their job that troubled porters; it was the racist attitudes that accompanied their work. Service work lends itself to social disdain and allows those who employ or benefit from servile workers to feel and act inherently superior to them. Perhaps this is a vestige of the Puritan foundations of the United States, wherein it was believed that wealth and material goods were the outward manifestation of God's favor. If one is a servant, and if one race seems always to be servants, the thinking goes, then perhaps there is some foreordained pattern to it all; perhaps there is something right about it. This type of thinking is largely rationalization, and is based on a self-fulfilling circular set of premises. If a race is subjugated and laws are enacted against its members, it is fatuous at best to point to that subjugation as a justification for its continuance. The Pullman Company attempted to equate service with second-class citizenship and acted as though it were being liberal and progressive in its policies toward its porters. The men themselves never accepted this, though it was difficult to avoid internalizing at least some of the racist propaganda they had been exposed to since birth about the inferiority of the black race.

The many narratives throughout this book are artifacts born of the struggle to work through the problems of identity, race, and occupation. They are attempts to sort it all out. Porters knew they were not children; they knew they worked hard and did not receive the wages white workers received. They knew they were the recipients of the aggression of the occasional mean-spirited passenger or the threatened conductor. They knew they were not any of these things, and they built their sense of identity, both personal and social, in part in opposition to these negative stereotypes.[17] For instance, as regards the rendering of their services, L. C. Richie and "Happy" Davis speak strongly and eloquently as they contrast the legitimate giving of service with the stigma of "Uncle Tomming."

L. C. Richie:

Anything that you can do, you can do with your head up.
It's what you think of yourself. If you think you are an
Uncle Tom, you are an Uncle Tom. Whether you're a
Pullman porter or whatever you are. So I never thought that
I was an Uncle Tom.

Lawrence W. (Happy) Davis:

Well, now, that's my philosophy. To get along with people
with a smile. A smile, that don't mean you're an Uncle Tom.

You're meeting a man on an equal basis. Your right hand of fellowship means so much, you know. But Tomming? No way.

L. C. Richie adds:

Another thing. When the passenger comes in and the first thing is he wants to grin, he's smiling and he's pleasant, you can be pleasant with him without "grinning," as we call it. You can treat him nice without that. You don't *have* to do that. And if he's going to tip me because I'm going to grin, I *don't need* it, and *don't want* it. But if he tips me because of my *service*, that's what I'm there for. To give him that service.[18]

To many of the porters, the job was, despite all of its negative aspects, an opportunity. If we have been looking at the "porter" as a category of occupational worker, we have also been listening to the voices of many individuals. These voices carry group concerns, group considerations, and group aesthetics, to be sure, but they are also the medium of personal stories and life histories. Jeff Todd Titon has suggested that life stories are, like personal experience narratives, a genre of their own. He says in this regard, "Life story-telling is a fiction, a making, an ordered past imposed by a present personality upon a disordered life."[19] In this he follows James Olney, who describes autobiography as an "impulse to order,"[20] and Patricia Spacks, who writes about literary autobiographies, suggesting that they are best approached as fictions, that is, creations based on the whole of one's past.[21] The same is true for folk autobiography as well, in much the same way as the occupational narratives are folk history. Seen in this way, the job of Pullman porter takes place as a long and meaningful chapter in lives that are otherwise varied. In those lives, men worked hard, left their wives and families for extended periods of time, and earned the means for their children and grandchildren to rise in society economically and to overcome the stereotypes of race and class. This chapter ends with one such story by Mr. Hunter Johnson:

When I left home, I sold my cows, my mules, and I pinned my money to my drawers. And we came across the Fourteenth Street Bridge there [from Virginia into Washington, D.C.], and I said, "I still got it." I paid the truck driver off when I got to my house. Then I started on the road years later. I would save my quarters and fifty cents and I went to the bank with four hundred dollars. I started a little bank account—*my own*. So I really thought it was a wonderful job. Because I had a sister teaching school, and she borrowed from me many times. I could let her have it. I felt *proud* to let her have it.[22]

Mr. Johnson's story is similar to that of C. L. Dellums, in chapter 1. Ultimately, porters took pride in their own, ostensibly small, accomplishments, and they are the heroes of their own stories— very human heroes.

NOTES

1. Jeff Todd Titon, *Early Downhome Blues: A Musical and Cultural Analysis* (Urbana: University of Illinois Press, 1977).

2. *The Girl in the Pullman*, DeMille Pictures, 1927. This film, unlike others mentioned below, is not catalogued in the Library of Congress.

3. Norm Cohen, *Long Steel Rail: The Railroad in American Folksong* (Urbana: University of Illinois Press, 1981), 535.

4. Ibid.

5. Ibid.

6. Howard Odum and Guy Johnson, *Negro Workaday Songs* (Chapel Hill, N.C.: University of North Carolina Press, 1926), 186–87.

7. *The Hold-Up of the Rocky Mountain Express*, Blackhawk Films, is catalogued in the Library of Congress Motion Picture Division as #FAA 3958.

8. *The Emperor Jones*, 1933, LC #FCA 6017–18.

9. Alex Haley, *Roots* (Garden City, N.Y.: Doubleday, 1976).

10. James MacPherson, *Hue and Cry* (Boston: Little Brown, 1969).

11. Octavus Roy Cohen, *Epic Peters, Pullman Porter* (New York, 1930).

12. Sinclair Lewis, *Babbit* (New York: New American Library, [1924] 1980), 120–21.

13. Hunter Johnson, July 12, 1983.

14. Rex Stewart, November 14, 1980.

15. Alan C. Speight, July 1, 1982.

16. Hunter Johnson, July 12, 1983.

17. See Alan Dundes, "Defining Identity through Folklore," in Anita Jacobson-Widding, ed., 235–61. See also Edward H. Spicer, "Persistent Cultural Systems: A Comparative Study of Identity Systems That Can Adapt to Contrasting Environments," *Science* 174 (1971): 795–800.

18. Lawrence W. Davis and Leroy C. Richie, November 14, 1980.

19. Jeff Todd Titon, "The Life Story," *Journal of American Folklore* 93 (1980): 290.

20. James Olney, *Metaphors of Self: The Meaning of Autobiography* (Princeton, N.J.: Princeton University Press, 1972), 3.

21. Patricia Spacks, *Imagining a Self: Autobiography and Novel in Eighteenth-Century England* (Cambridge, Mass.: Harvard University Press, 1976).

22. Hunter Johnson, July 12, 1983.

In 1925, in an Elks Lodge in Harlem, the Brotherhood of Sleeping Car Porters was born. Note the motto "Fight or Be Slaves" on the union flag. *Schomburg Center, New York Public Library*

Brotherhood of Sleeping Car Porters negotiating team, 1937. *Left to right:* L. O. Manson, Bennie Smith, Ashley L. Totten, T. T. Patterson, A. Philip Randolph, Milton P. Webster, C. L. Dellums, and E. J. Bradley. *Schomburg Center, New York Public Library*

Brotherhood of Sleeping Car Porters march. *Chicago Historical Society, ICHi-15800*

E. D. Nixon and Rosa Parks in 1955, after Rosa Parks had been arrested for breaking segregation laws. Nixon organized the Montgomery Bus Boycott as a result. *Wide World Photos*

A. Philip Randolph at the 1963 March on Washington, which he organized.
Wide World Photos

During wartime, Pullman cars were used to carry soldiers across the country. Porters were pressed into round-the-clock service. These publicity shots depict the increased volume of work the porters faced. Courtesy of the *Library of Congress*

Note the letter D on the sole of the boot. Porters often identified footwear in such a way to allow them to shine more than one pair at a time. *Courtesy of the Library of Congress*

Porters smiled when performing their service role, but when they were "offstage," they showed signs of weariness and strain. *Courtesy of the Library of Congress*

Early promotional photo depicting newlyweds. The porter stifles a giggle over the upside-down magazine. *Courtesy of Santa Fe Railway*

A 1943 Pullman Company depiction of a porter as enthusiastic, eager to please, and childish. *Courtesy of the Library of Congress*

Note the "body language" in this publicity still: the porter is shown in a position of inferiority and submission. *Courtesy of the Pullman Collection, The Newberry Library, Chicago*

Graphic renditions of porters in promotional materials showed them as having Caucasian features. *Courtesy of the Pullman Collection, The Newberry Library, Chicago*

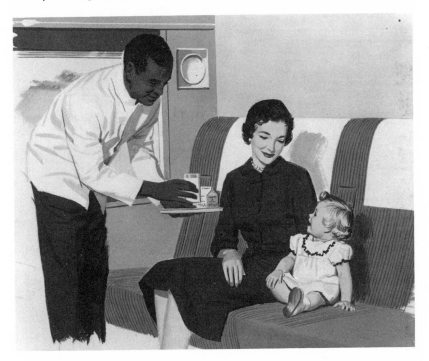

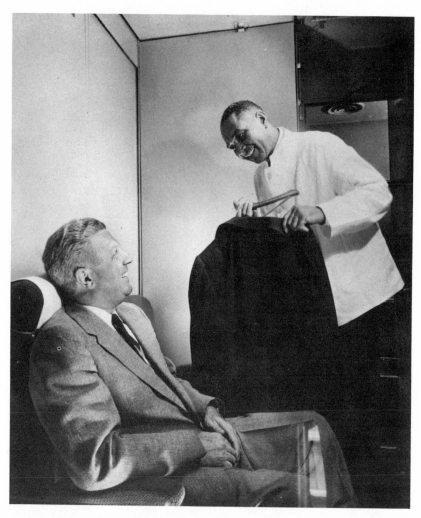

Porters took pride in the service they provided for their passengers. *Courtesy of the Pullman Collection, The Newberry Library, Chicago*

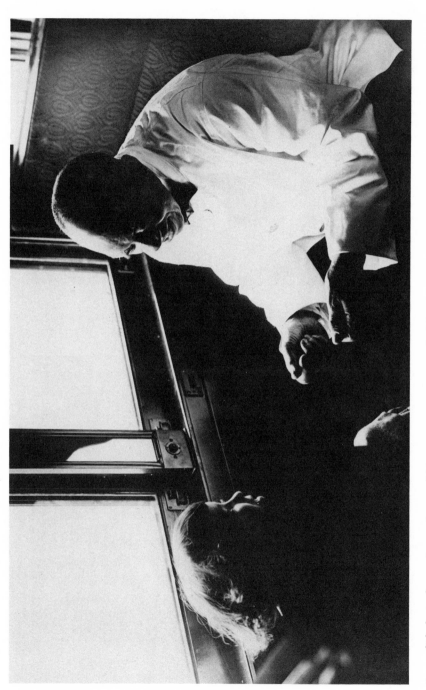

A candid shot of a porter and one of his young passengers. Smithsonian Institution Photo No. 222173

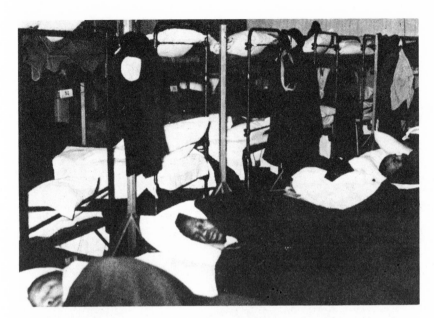

Porters sleeping in quarters provided for them by the Pullman Company. Although crowded, the porters made the best of their situation. *Courtesy of the Library of Congress*

Often they played card games such as bid whist throughout the night. *Courtesy of the Library of Congress*

6. The End of the Line

Pullman porters helped each other and covered for each other while on the train and fraternized with each other while off. Their brotherhood was bonded by more than the necessity to unionize, and their fraternity was established out of something more than convenience. Their occupation is at the core of their identity, as to this day they perceive each other and identify themselves as Pullman porters. Ultimately, the porters were an enclaved group, despite the fact that they traveled so far and saw so much. A Pullman porter was by definition a black man and a servant: a minority, segregated, restricted occupationally. All of the multiple factors of their identity coalesced in their job. Occupation and life are close to conflated in these cases; that is why the occupational identity persists after the job is gone.[1]

At the end of a line, when the train arrived in a city, porters stayed in quarters provided by the Pullman Company. Sometimes these were in hotels, but more often they were beds rented in seedy rooming houses or in a YMCA. Old Pullman cars too debilitated to continue in use might also be used, cars that Leon Long describes as "particularly fixed" for porters:

> Sometimes they'd park some cars out on the track and make them hotel rooms. Some years ago. They were *rotten*. They were the cars that were about wore out. They wouldn't use them cars out on the line. You'd have to stay on the cars unless you had money or were able to go somewhere and rent a room.[2]

The quarters may have been shabby, but the porters managed to turn a disadvantageous situation into a vital and joyous event. At the quarters, during layovers, the porters *played*. Old friendships were renewed, new friendships cemented. News was spread, of the union, of life on the line. One would think that after a run of perhaps six days or even more, porters would not be anxious to spend their off hours with other porters. Indeed, if they happened to have friends in the town in which they were staying, or if they could afford to rent a hotel room, they might seek alternative lodging. Nevertheless, porters preferred the company of each other, since it was only other porters who understood them and their experiences. Porters have fond memories of times spent during layovers; much of their camaraderie was developed during these periods. Freed from the pressures of work, layovers offered porters a time to relax and enjoy themselves. At some of the larger quarters, there were so many porters that the time took on a festive atmosphere. Leon Long describes it:

> When you got off your car you went to the quarters. There'd be maybe a couple hundred porters, maybe, in a place like New York, gathered around in groups, laughing, telling tales, playing cards.
> Porters act like brothers. If you saw a uniform, you felt like you had a friend. All those porters be together from different districts. You might be in New York, you'd have Kansas City porters, Tampa porters, Jacksonville porters, Boston porters, and sometimes the porters were going in all directions and from everywhere. California, San Diego, down there. We have porters sometimes from conventions, going to inaugurations sometimes. There'd be thousands of porters you'd be coming in contact with, hauling people.[3]

William Harrington:

> We played cards and checkers in the quarters. Those that wasn't out looking for women was in the quarters. We'd play cards, we'd just have a big time playing cards and checkers. That was our main object in laying over. Bid whist. That was the most *prominent* game going, that was the most *prominent* game going with *all* porters. Very seldom anybody'd gamble. But that bid whist, checkers, everybody's raising hell playing cards. I know I learned how to *play* with porters. We talked more about women than anything else.[4]

Leon Long continues:

> All of these crews worked together on different trains. Maybe you get five or six Pullman cars on there, and every car you got a porter on there. Well, most of the time, that crew gets together, maybe stops at the same quarters, the same Y, the same hotel, or the same whatever. Conditions in some quarters, you're mostly grouped together. Everywhere you go, you had a different crew this time, different crew next time. You all get together; if you all work out of the

same district, you're on the same train. Like here, I go to work here, four or five porters, we'd be running down to Florida. There'd be four or five porters out of this district. There'd be a couple of cars coming out of New York, when they get to Washington, they'd hook them cars up on the same train. You might get to Richmond, they'd put on another car. Well, you got a Richmond porter, the Washington porters, the New York porters are on the same train. Maybe most of you stop at the same quarters.[5]

The feelings of fraternity and even *communitas*[6] that derived from these large-scale layovers resulted in organized recreations that involved teamwork. Porters' *work* was essentially solitary, since each porter was responsible for his own car, and even though porters systematically aided each other so as to allow a man to get some sleep or covered for each other when one got sick, each porter worked by himself and raised tips for himself. His recreation, on the other hand, was social. Along with card playing, porters participated in other group-oriented pastimes such as baseball and singing. A group of singers was always called a quartet, no matter how many men were involved in it. All of these activities, interestingly enough, were based on group participation, especially the singing, which was harmonic.

Conversational storytelling, a major leisure activity, had its own unarticulated rules in which men took turns contributing their own narratives. Likewise, so did their favored card game, bid whist, which was more formally structured and rule-ordered, and so on through group singing and team sports such as baseball games. Moreover, for all their card playing, the porters testify that they gambled little, a fact that I have noticed when witnessing card games in a variety of contexts, including individuals' homes and after business meetings. Perhaps the attraction of gambling was satisfied by the nature of the tipping system, wherein every run was a gamble of sorts, and every interaction with every passenger a game. Whatever the case, porters found pleasure during their layovers and at other times as well by engaging in structured, fictive interactions with other porters. William D. Miller, followed by others, describes some of these activities:

Pullman porters, after the run was over and they got back to the quarters, the place that they stayed, they might play a little bid whist and sing in a quartet.

Ernest Ford, Jr.:

We used to travel long distances, say for instance hauling soldiers, say from Washington, D.C., to California. And we would *deadhead* back to Washington. Now, deadheading means we would be in a private car by ourselves, a sleeping car, just coming back to Washington to get another assignment. And of course, in the course of that deadhead, yes, we would get together and sing, make music that way, yes. There would be a group of us, say, seventeen porters, say four of them would get over there and start a song, try to quartet, try to sing a song or try to imitate some of the other singers such as the Mills Brothers or the Ink Spots, that sort of thing.

C. J. Talley:

They had quartets, used to go around and entertain. They was local. Each district, you know. Like Washington, they had a quartet. And they would meet, entertain, at some official's (or wherever they go) engagements. They would meet once a year and get a prize. Each district used to get "Best Quartet" or "Musician." And they all had their own musicians along with the quartets.

L. C. Richie:

I remember when they had quartets. That was back in the twenties. They had baseball teams, too. Districts had baseball teams, and they would compete against the waiters, and the other districts and all of that.

Lawrence W. Davis sums it up:

Porters used to have a whole lot of good times.[7]

Of all these activities, card playing was by far the most accessible and the most widespread. When porters played cards, the game of choice was most often bid whist, so much so that they refer to it as "the porters' game," and they will tell you that it was invented by porters to help pass the time. Like the storytelling, the card playing is itself a traditional event, and it is an occasion for storytelling and other kinds of binding talk. It is not, however, simply an excuse to talk. Unlike, for instance, an otherwise similar description of a pastime in Nova Scotia, described by Richard Bauman,[8] the card game here is a primary focus of attention and activity. Narrative ceases when the bid whist playing begins.

Being deeply rooted in the work-play cycles of the porters' job, the game has become an extension of their identity. They believe that it was born of the layover and served an important purpose promoting communality and smooth interaction in a situation in which they were insulated from society because of segregation and hostility. They went from being servant-hosts on the Pullman cars, where they interacted with powerful businessmen and politicians, to the in-group orientation of the Pullman quarters. Like their work, their play was consistent with their aesthetic of individuality within community cooperation. On the job, along with the reciprocal co-operation when covering for each other, they left each other alone, saying, "You don't bother my stations, and I don't bother yours," since any infringement on another porter's territory was economically threatening and would be considered a hostile act. Likewise, they play together in a group, in teams of two men with a crowd of porters looking on, admiring, encouraging, responding; for example, the card game becomes a spectator sport. Within that structure they compete as individuals, and a great deal of honor and status is given to the recognized master player. Significantly, the same kind of structure and aesthetic of individuals joining together in a team, in friendly competition with other such teams, is present in the quartet singing and the baseball playing.

Not surprisingly, then, stories are told about marathon card games. In a sense, these stories are much like the heroic legends of a "golden age," since they depict the porter's world as dangerous, spontaneous, exciting, almost swashbuckling. These stories do not deal with life on the train, either good or bad, but rather, with life *off* the train, and the fun had between runs.

Fred Fair:

> We played cards, we played checkers, after we'd get up, after a little rest. It was always enjoyable, but the card game was the main thing. The boys would rush to bed and get up to start the game. We played four days and four nights, coming in from California, once. There was four of us and we just settled in one car and played cards all the way. Get up in the morning, eat breakfast, and start right in playing just like we was going to work. We were deadheading. Well, I was a winner. I was this kind of player. Give me an equal break and I'd win more games than I'd lose—and what I mean by that, if I could get a player as good as yours to play with me. So I did, I won more games than I lost.
>
> All these men were good. This boy Richie, nobody could beat Richie. We used to play down in Q Street [the old union headquarters], and Richie and I, well, Richie's *good*,

no question about it. But like I say, give me an equal break and I'll play them just like I play anybody else, and I'll win some, too. *Miller's* a good card player. But I'll tell you, Richie's better. It's just how you play your hand and what you get out of your hand. So many times you have a good hand and play it bad and don't get what you should out of them. It's not that you *win* all the time, but it's just how you play. Like I say, you might have a bad partner, and you just can't *beat* two good men with a bad partner.

Davis is a good card player, too. He's a good player. And Ford's a good player. He's not in a class with Richie or Miller, but he's a good player. I used to play down on Q Street every Wednesday. I would open up a lot of times, before the secretary even got there. We'd start playing and play to 3:30, 4:00, every time. The *best* card player I ever met was a fella named *Breeder.* Breeder, he lived in Chicago, and it's between Breeder and a fella from Oklahoma City. We always used to meet in Chicago every five days and we played. And this Breeder, he's good. But one thing about his boy Wesley (he ran out of Oklahoma City), only thing about him, he's got a memory. He could take a—if you're playing trumps, he'd take a trey and pick up your deuce anytime out of your hand. But that was just too *fine. I* couldn't get down that fine. So those two was the best I ever saw. But there were some good ones.[9]

There still are some "good ones." Although the occupation no longer exists, the men still gather together to play bid whist. It is at these meetings that they also share stories with each other, performing their identities as porters, and go over the events that shaped them over the years. Both the storytelling and the card games offer porters the opportunity to exhibit their own personal style within the framework of the group event. During these all-male events, no wives are present. When the games are held in the home of a married man, his wife retires early. If she returns at all, it is only to say goodnight. She is not expected, nor does she expect, to be a participant in the evening's activities. At such times as these, when the men are talking of marathon card games and master players, they might also remark upon those of their colleagues who demonstrated remarkable skill in the execution of their work. Fred Fair, who worked cars for Presidents Roosevelt and Truman, approaches this subject when he tells how he had his own distinctive style for making beds. The pride he took in his work is evident in his words:

There were some *fast* men, no question about that. And
good men, I mean, they could make a good bed, regulation
and good. I wasn't bad myself. Our superintendent came
through the President's train one night and had an assistant
with him. When they got to my car, this was the third car in
the train, so when they came in the door, I was working in
the middle of the car in the room somewhere. So I heard the
superintendent, he was talking very loud and he told his
assistant, "Fair's in this car somewhere." So the assistant
superintendent said, "No, Fair's back on the other car, way
back." He said, "Well, how do you know he's in here?" He
said, "Well, that's his bed. Don't you know his bed when
you see it?"

So, I can make a pretty good bed. On the *specials*, I kind
of get away from the old Pullman. I'd make a—kind of make
it a little different. I'd always try to get good linen, so you
could *make* a pretty bed. But he recognized it. I'd fold it
back a little bit different. You know, the old Pullman fold,
everybody knows that, whoever rode in a Pullman car. But I
made my folds a little bit different. I try to fix it so it had a
handle on the fold, where you could just catch it and pull it
right over you.

There was one man in Cincinnati, he and his brother,
both of them were famous for being fast. But there were a
lot of fast men around. Like I say, I wasn't too bad myself.
But these two boys could, I believe, they could beat me. The
boy was named Fence.[10]

Leroy Shackleford recalls:

The fastest man I knew of was a fella here in Chicago by the
name of Wynne. He's dead now. This guy, he drank all the
time. Every time you saw him, he came to work full of
liquor, and he kept Listerine. You couldn't smell anything
but Listerine. When he would get back from his run, he was
running to Minneapolis, and he would get in in the morning,
the train would get in at seven o'clock, and they stayed in
the station for half an hour, you know. Passengers would get
off and after his last passenger would get off, he'd get off.
And he had to put away all those beds. And he was the only
guy in the district who could get off the car at that rate of
speed. I didn't know of anybody else who could do that. I've
heard them talk of others, but I didn't know them.[11]

Interestingly, I am often asked why the porters' stories do not reflect more of the underside of life on the road, why there are not more tales of heavy drinkers or of prostitutes. Surely such an underside existed, but the fact is, most alcoholics probably would not have been able to keep up with the work, and so would not have survived long as Pullman porters. That is why the story of the heavy drinker who did good work is told: he is a notable exception. As regards prostitutes, the men were not saints and do not pretend to be. Perhaps they avoided telling me much about this subject in an effort to maintain their positive image, but the truth is that many of the men were quite moral and did not frequent prostitutes. At the very least, stories of these matters do not form a large portion of their narrative repertoire. The expectation that porters led a wild, illicit life off the job may in fact be another racial stereotype.

The men who play these games and who tell these tales—the men and women who have helped create this book with their words and their lives—are now elderly. Many have passed away; others are still vital and remain contemporary in the best sense of that word. They are glorious in their age. Failing health, disease, and inevitable death are only the latest in a lifelong series of challenges to respond to. They resist being relics; they refuse to relinquish their vitality. Although they are living treasures, they are not antiques, and it has not been my intention to portray them as such.

Nevertheless, the Pullman cars no longer run, and the era of the Pullman porter is over. The company went out of business in 1969; the Brotherhood of Sleeping Car Porters became a division of the much larger Brotherhood of Railway and Airline Clerks in 1978, and in 1979, A. Philip Randolph died. Those men who survive have faced and overcome their greatest challenges. But they continue to think of themselves as Pullman porters and to associate with other Pullman porters. The occupation was and still is a primary basis on which they establish their personal identities. They *are* Pullman porters: the identity transcends employment; it has become all-encompassing. Their job was both good and bad in its various aspects, but no matter how difficult the bad parts were, the porters never let them eclipse the good.

Albert Camus, the famous French writer, has said that "without work, life loses meaning. But when work is without soul, all life stifles and dies." These men were hardworking and ambitious. Today they look at their accomplishments with pride, at their homes and their college-educated children, and they are proud of the

Brotherhood of Sleeping Car Porters. They still revere the uniform, and when asked how they feel about their identities as porters, they answer enthusiastically in the positive.

The fact that these men are still perceived as Pullman porters, by each other and by others as well, continues to affect their lives and to contribute to new stories of recent experiences. In 1981, for instance, Happy Davis left Washington, D.C., to live for a time in Cincinnati, where he had a porter friend. Upon arriving in town, he went looking for temporary lodging until he got settled. An attractive complex of housing units for senior citizens caught his eye, so he inquired as to vacancies. Happy continues:

> The girl at the counter told me there were none. No vacancies. I said, "Oh, man, I need a place. I'm a retired Pullman porter in town to visit my friend, and I don't have anywhere to stay." And this was, you know, housing for the elderly, senior citizens. Well, the manager turned around when I said I was a Pullman porter. He heard me say "Pullman porter" and he said, "If you're a Pullman porter, you're my man!" And he shook my hand. Because he used to ride the *Pullman* cars, see, and he said to that girl, "You find him something."
>
> And you know how many apartments they had empty? Fifty! But they didn't want me in there because I was black. But when he found out I was a Pullman porter, well then, it was a different story. All because I was a Pullman porter. That's the kind of thing the job has done for me.[12]

As Mr. Glenn said earlier, working for the Pullman Company was both a good job and a bad job. He was commenting on the essential duality of the job. Simply put, it was an available job, which made it good, but it was an abusive job, which made it bad. Other porters also perceived this dichotomy, often by making the distinction between the socializing, the card playing, the camaraderie, in short, the folklife of the job and the unfair system they labored within. The community aspects of the job were good, the inequalities were bad. Mr. Davis is fond of referring to the job as "miles of smiles." Explaining the term, he says:

> That's what the Pullman Company wanted from us, miles of smiles. But I remember lots of funny stories. See, I had fun out there, a lot of fun. Miles of smiles and satisfied passengers all the way. Yes sir, that's what we had: *miles of smiles!*[13]

Again, the statement of dichotomy; again, the resolution of a duality: the Pullman Company wanted subservience, sublimation of personal identity, submission, the kind of smiles the porters call grins, what Ernest Ford describes as "the blackest man with the whitest teeth." Lawrence W. "Happy" Davis, resorting to the classic trickster mode of reversal, gives the company exactly that: miles of smiles redefined as rich, vital enjoyment, personal engagement, pride and pleasure—fun—from the job. The company wanted grins; the porters had, finally, the last laugh. This was the minimum response to the situation. Total rejection and confrontation was the maximum.

A final piece of testimony comes from the end of a long night's socializing after a hard day's work on the documentary film featuring the porters. Mr. Ford turned to the camera, so he was consciously performing, but his words were spontaneous and unrehearsed. He perfectly and poetically summarized the series of dualities and ambiguities that porters perceive in their own self-images, and the good humor by which they are able to reconcile the opposites into a single greater persona: "I'd like to make a pronouncement," he began.

You can see, we are all men of the first magnitude,
We are always able to look through muddy water and
    see dry land,
As you can see, we know the answers to all the problems,
As you can see, we are orators,
And we owe it all to A. Philip Randolph.
Also, we are clowns, in a sense,
And we are gentlemen.
Thank you very much, and God bless.[14]

NOTES

1. See Karmela Liebkind, in Anita Jacobson-Widding, ed., Identity.

2. Leon Long, July 7, 1982.

3. Ibid.

4. William Harrington, July 16, 1982.

5. Leon Long, July 7, 1982.

6. Victor Turner, "Betwixt and Between: The Liminal Period in Rites de Passage," in The Forest of Symbols (Ithaca, N.Y.: Cornell University Press, 1967).

7. Lawrence W. Davis, Ernest Ford, Jr., William D. Miller, and Clarence J. Talley, November 15, 1980.

8. Richard Bauman, "The LaHave Island General Store: Sociability and Verbal Art in a Nova Scotia Community," *Journal of American Folklore* 85 (1972): 330–43.

9. Fred Fair, March 30, 1983.

10. Ibid.

11. Leroy Shackleford, November 5, 1983.

12. Lawrence W. Davis, December 8, 1986.

13. Lawrence W. Davis, July 1, 1978.

14. Ernest Ford, Jr., November 15, 1980.

Appendix: List of Interviews

Most of the material in this book was collected in interviews I have conducted with retired Pullman porters since 1978. The first interviews were done one-on-one in the homes of the individual men. Each of these sessions lasted between one and two hours, and most of the men were remarkably open about life on the railroad, considering it was our first meeting. In the many years since then, I have interviewed many of the same individuals in a variety of circumstances: in their homes, in my home, singly, and in groups. On some occasions, the Washington porters have met in my home for a night of card playing; I was fortunate enough to record extended narrative sessions on these occasions (such as the one on passengers dying). In Chicago and New York, I attended meetings of the retired porters' groups. I interviewed men at the scene of these meetings and some in their homes as well. Mr. E. D. Nixon I spoke with by telephone on three occasions before meeting with him and interviewing him in Washington, D.C. He had come to visit his nephew in Baltimore. We arranged for an interview, and we were able to film an interview segment for the documentary film. Similarly, I interviewed Mr. C. L. Dellums in Washington while making the film. Based on my fieldwork, I attempted to recreate the narrative sessions both at museum and festival settings, and for the film as well. Often during these public sessions, the porters would tell stories I had not heard before, so they too served as a source of data.

This data elicited in public sessions needs to be addressed. To what extent did the porters "clean up" the material in order to put on a proper face? In general, how much did the fact that they were being interviewed by a younger white man affect the situation or inhibit the data, even when these interviews were done in their homes? That these various factors did affect the data can be taken for granted; we know that context is a primary dimension of any communicative act (see, for instance, Dell Hymes, "Breakthrough into Performance," in Dan Ben-Amos and Kenneth S. Goldstein, eds., *Folklore: Performance and Communication* [The Hague: Mouton, 1975]; and my own "Occupational Ghostlore: Social Context and the Expression of Belief," *Journal of American Folklore* 101 [1988], 400.) Over the years, however, I have had a chance to listen to many different stories, many different conversations. Men often disagree with each other over such major issues as just exactly how bad it was out there. W. D. Miller continually reminded me that one man's experience was not necessarily another's; in his case, I suspect that he was attempting to project a positive image. Overall, however, as I witnessed men debating fine points and, ultimately, negotiating their cultural reality in many different situations, the stories contained in this volume continually emerged as culturally true.

On three occasions, in 1978, 1983, and 1984, I conducted public workshops with the porters at the Smithsonian Institution's Festival of American Folklife. Those sessions were tape-recorded, and the tapes are stored in the Smithsonian Institution's Office of Folklife Programs Archives. A complete record of all interviews conducted during the making of the ethnographic documentary film *Miles of Smiles, Years of Struggle: The Untold Story of the Black Pullman Porter*, by Jack Santino and Paul R. Wagner (Benchmark Films, 1982), is also in the archives of the Office of Folklife Programs, along with footage shot but not used in the final cut of the film.

Several interviews were conducted with the aid and assistance of Carl Fleischhauer and equipment on loan from the American Folklife Center at the Library of Congress. Reel-to-reel tapes of those interviews are the property of the Folklife Center and will be placed in the Archive of Folk Culture at the Library of Congress.

Not all interviews were tape-recorded. Some were notated with pencil and paper, especially the earliest ones. In other cases, I would be told important information or interesting stories at a time when I was unprepared or unable to record or otherwise note them. On more than one occasion, I attempted to take notes while driving a van through city streets, while the men were enjoying themselves and entertaining each other in the back with humorous stories. I do not believe I have ever had a conversation with a porter, including telephone conversations, in which I did not find myself wishing I could record it. In some cases, then, no recorded document exists.

Following is a list of interviews. Material which is housed at the Smithsonian Institution's Office of Folklife Programs is noted as SIFP, followed by specific accession numbers. Those which are the property of the American Folklife Center are noted as LC AFC.

Samuel Beasley	August 18, 1980
George Bee	July 12, 1980
Troy Braille	November 4, 1982
	November 5, 1983
Charles Bremmer, A. Philip Randolph Institute	July 13, 1980
	August 19, 1980
Granderson Bush	August 18, 1980
Walter (King) Cole	May 18, 1980
	November 12, 1980
	October 8, 1983
Lawrence W. (Happy) Davis	May 11, 1978
	July 1, 1978

	October 5, 1978, SIFP 1978 088
	" " " SIFP 1978 089
	October 6, 1978, SIFP 1978 094
	" " " SIFP 1978 095
	May 5, 1980
	November 14–15, 1980
	May 26, 1982
	June 1, 1982
	June 6, 1982
	January 7, 1983
	January 17, 1983
	January 24, 1983
	February 7, 1983
	June 26, 1983, SIFP CT 120
	June 27, 1983, SIFP CT 123
	July 2, 1983, SIFP CT 133
	July 3, 1983, SIFP CT 134
	June 27, 1984
	June 29, 1984
	July 1, 1984
	July 5, 1984
	July 7, 1984
	December 8, 1986
C. L. Dellums	November 13, 1980
	November 16, 1980
	November 17, 1980
Congressman Ronald Dellums	November 16, 1980
	November 17, 1980
Fred Fair	March 30, 1983, LC AFC
Ernest Ford, Jr.	May 1, 1978
	July 2, 1978
	September 11, 1978
	October 5, 1978, SIFP 1978 088
	" " " SIFP 1978 089
	October 6, 1978, SIFP 1978 094
	" " " SIFP 1978 095
	May 4, 1980
	November 14, 1980
	November 15, 1980
	November 5, 1981
	May 26, 1982
	June 1, 1982
	June 6, 1982
	November 4, 1982

	November 24, 1983
	June 26, 1983, SIFP 1983 CT120
	June 27, 1983, SIFP 1983 CT123
	July 2, 1983, SIFP 1983 CT133
	July 3, 1983, SIFP 1983 CT134
	June 27, 1984
	June 29, 1984
	July 1, 1984
	July 5, 1984
	July 7, 1984
Green Glenn	May 11, 1978
	October 5, 1978, SIFP 1978 088
	" " " SIFP 1978 089
	April, 1980
	May 5, 1980
	November 18, 1980
	May 6, 1982
Homer Glenn	July 13, 1980
	August 18, 1980
	November 13, 1980
	November 14, 1980
Leslie H. Green	July 12, 1980
William Harrington	May 2, 1980
	November 12, 1980
	July 16, 1982, LC AFC
Hunter Johnson	July 12, 1983, LC AFC
Lafayette Linton	July 12, 1980
Leon Long	November 12, 1980
	July 7, 1982, LC AFC
Benjamin McLauren	July 11, 1980
	August 17, 1980
William D. Miller	May 6, 1978
	October 5, 1978, SIFP 1978 088
	" " " SIFP 1978 089
	October 6, 1978, SIFP 1978 094
	" " " SIFP 1978 095
	April 3, 1980
	May 26, 1982
	June 1, 1982
	June 6, 1982
	June 26, 1983, SIFP 1983 CT 120
	June 27, 1983, SIFP 1983 CT 123

	July 2, 1983, SIFP 1983 CT 133
	July 3, 1983, SIFP 1983 CT 134
	June 27, 1984
	June 29, 1984
	July 1, 1984
	July 5, 1984
	July 7, 1984
Gus Morrison	August 8, 1982
E. D. Nixon	February 25, 1981
	May 27, 1981
	July 14, 1981
Leroy C. Richie	May 8, 1978
	October 5, 1978, SIFP 1978 088
	" " " SIFP 1978 089
	October 6, 1978, SIFP 1978 094
	" " " SIFP 1978 095
	April 7, 1980
	November 14, 1980
	November 15, 1980
	May 6, 1982
	November 4, 1982
	January 24, 1983
	June 26, 1983, SIFP 1983 CT 120
	June 27, 1983, SIFP 1983 CT 123
	July 2, 1983, SIFP 1983 CT 133
	July 3, 1983, SIFP 1983 CT 134
	June 27, 1984
	June 29, 1984
	July 1, 1984
	July 5, 1984
	July 7, 1984
Leroy Shackleford	May 16, 1980
	November 5, 1983
J. D. Shaw	May 6, 1978
	April 25, 1980
	May 6, 1980
A. C. Speight	July 1, 1982, LC AFC
Rex Stewart	May 17, 1980
	November 13, 1980
	November 14, 1980

Clarence J. Talley   May 3, 1978
                                                November 15, 1980

Rosina Coruthers Tucker   June 19, 1981
                                                May 26, 1982
                                                June 1, 1982
                                                June 6, 1982
                                                November 4, 1982
                                                January 24, 1983
                                                May 21, 1984
                                                June 27, 1984
                                                June 29, 1984
                                                July 1, 1984
                                                July 2, 1984
                                                July 5, 1984
                                                July 7, 1984
                                                December 15, 1986

Johnny L. Williams   August 18, 1980

Resources

Other than the many interviews with Mrs. Tucker and the porters, certain archives and institutions have been most important in the realization of this project. Perhaps the richest source of information on the Brotherhood of Sleeping Car Porters is the personal archival collection belonging to Mr. Benjamin McLauren. Mr. McLauren is a former porter and union division chief in New York. His extensive collection of papers and photographs is housed at the Bronx Community College and also stored in his home. In addition, the Schomberg Center of the New York Public Library in Harlem has some important materials, mostly photographic, on black life and labor in the early part of this century, including Pullman porters. The same is true of the National Archives in Washington, D.C.

The records of the Brotherhood of Sleeping Car Porters and some personal papers of A. Philip Randolph (approximately 31,000 items) are housed in the Manuscripts Division of the Library of Congress. Most of this material dates from after 1950. The photographs in this collection are housed in the Prints and Photographs Division of the Library of Congress. A collection of some 11,400 items concerning A. Philip Randolph was received by the Library of Congress in 1984. At the time of this writing, they were unprocessed. The Manuscripts Division also houses the papers of the National Association for the Advancement of Colored People and the National Urban League.

Mr. Leroy Shackleford is currently head of the Brotherhood of Sleeping Car Porters Division of the Brotherhood of Railway and Airline Clerks in Chicago. He generously opened those records of the Brotherhood that are in his possession to me. Many valuable records from the Brotherhood's pre-1950 period are in the Chicago Historical Society Library and Manuscripts Division. The Newberry Library, also in Chicago, houses the archives of the Pullman Company and has a great many valuable photographs and audiotapes documenting Brotherhood meetings. The Newberry Library also has a collection of Pullman scrapbooks with many rare papers and articles, and it owns copies of the *Pullman Porter Review* and *Pullman News*, both company publications. A. Philip Randolph's address to a meeting of the Brotherhood quoted in this book was transcribed from a cassette tape provided by the Chicago Historical Society.

Secondary sources of historical materials include such institutions as the Bancroft Library in Berkeley, California, which holds the BSCP Pacific Coast Division Papers in its Manuscripts Division. It is impossible, of course, to completely discuss the vast historical source materials on subjects as large as the Pullman Company and the founding of the Brotherhood of Sleeping Car Porters, as well as the civil rights movement in the 1950s and the BSCP's relationship to it.

Bibliographical Resources

Two books have been written about the Brotherhood of Sleeping Car Porters. The first, entitled *The Brotherhood of Sleeping Car Porters: Its Origins and Development*, by Brailsford R. Brazeal (New York: Harper and Brothers, 1946) is a pioneering effort which stood alone until the publication of *Keeping the Faith: A. Philip Randolph, Milton P. Webster, and the Brotherhood of Sleeping Car Porters 1925-1937*, by William Harris (Urbana: University of Illinois Press, 1978). Harris points out that Brazeal, an economist, was "more interested in the economic development of the union than its wider influences" (223). Harris seeks to correct this with his volume, and together with *A. Philip Randolph: A Biographical Portrait* by Jervis Anderson (New York: Harcourt Brace and Jovanovich, 1973), we now have a solid record of the years from the founding of the union to its recognition, and of A. Philip Randolph, its leader. A condensed version of these events is contained in chapter 4 of Harris's *The Harder We Run* (New York: Oxford University Press, 1982), 77–94, while Anderson's *This Was Harlem: A Cultural Portrait 1900-1950* (New York: Farrar, Straus & Giroux, 1981) gives a view of Randolph outside of Brotherhood activities.

These books are histories of the union or of its leader. *Miles of Smiles* features primarily firsthand interview material. Recollections about the union and the civil rights movement are included, but the book attempts to cover the entire occupational experience as it was lived by the rank-and-file porter. Essentially, the book adopts an anthropological perspective on American culture. The problems involved in doing this kind of fieldwork research have been discussed in many places elsewhere; a few titles that guide and instruct in folklore research specifically are worth mentioning. The first such fieldwork manual in folklore is Kenneth S. Goldstein's pioneering *A Guide for Fieldworkers in Folklore* (Hatboro, Pa.: Folklore Associates, 1964). More recent volumes include Edward D. Ives, *The Tape-Recorded Interview: A Manual for Fieldworkers in Folklore and Oral History* (Knoxville: University of Tennessee Press, 1980).

Barbara Allen and William Lynwood Montell, *From Memory to History: Sources in Local History Research* (Nashville: American Association for State and Local History, 1981) addresses important questions in oral history. Model historical studies done by these authors include William Lynwood Montell, *The Saga of Coe Ridge: A Study in Oral History* (Knoxville: University of Tennessee Press, 1970), and Edward D. Ives, *Joe Scott, the Woodsman Songmaker* (Urbana: University of Illinois Press, 1978).

Sandra Stahl has written extensively on the personal experience narrative as folklore, and I have followed her concept of traditional performance in this book. See her "The Personal Narrative as Folklore," *Journal of the Folklore Institute* 14, no. 102 (1977): 9–30. Richard Bauman's studies of verbal performances are set forth in his *Verbal Art as Performance* (Prospect Heights, Ill.: Waveland Press, Inc., 1984). Certainly Dan Ben-Amos's definition of folklore as artistic communication in small groups has informed this study in fundamental ways; see his "Toward a Definition of Folklore in Context" in Americo Paredes and Richard Bauman, eds., *New Perspectives in Folklore* (Austin: University of Texas Press, 1972), 3–16. Dell Hymes's article "Breakthrough into Performance" in *Folklore: Performance and Communication*, edited by Dan Ben-Amos and Kenneth S. Goldstein (The Hague: Mouton, 1975), 11–74, is a very important study of storytelling in casual conversation. The concept of "traditionalizing experience" is taken from Hymes's "Folklore's Nature and the Sun's Myth," *Journal of American Folklore* 88 (1975): 345–69. Also, see my own article "Miles of Smiles, Years of Struggle: The Negotiation of Black Occupational Identity through Personal Experience Narrative," *Journal of American Folklore* 96, no. 382 (1983): 393–412, for a structuralist approach to some of the material covered in this book.

First Person America, edited by Ann Banks (New York: Vintage Books, 1981), is a volume of excerpts from the vast collection of interviews done in the 1930s for the Works Progress Administration. Much of this collection is housed in the Archive of Folk Culture of the American Folklife Center in the Library of Congress. Banks includes a brief piece of testimony by a Pullman porter in her book, but the testimony is not about his occupation. More useful is the introduction to the volume, which includes a good short description of the WPA and a discussion of oral history interviewing as well. The history of the Pullman Company is best described in Stanley Buder's *Pullman: An Experiment in Industrial Order and Community Planning 1880–1930* (New York: Oxford University Press, 1967). Lawrence W. Levine's *Black Culture and Black Consciousness: Afro-American Folk Thought from Slavery to Freedom* (New York: Oxford University Press, 1977) is a triumph of interdisciplinary work. In it, the author explores several facets of black expressive culture, folk and popular. He also draws attention to the fact that porters mediated between rural and urban lifestyles by distributing phonograph records into rural areas (226). In this regard, see also Marshall W. Stearns, *The Story of Jazz* (New York: Oxford University Press, 1956), 167–68, Perry Bradford, *Born with the Blues: Perry Bradford's Own Story* (New York: Oak Publications, 1965), 48, and W. C. Handy, *Father of the Blues: An Autobiography* (New York: Collier Books, 1970).

There are many studies of black expressive culture. Works by black folklorists such as J. Mason Brewer, *Worser Days and Better Times* (Chicago: Quadrangle Books, 1965); Arthur Huff Fauset, "Negro Folktales from the South (Alabama, Mississippi, Louisiana)," *Journal of American Folklore* 40 (1927): 211–78; and Zora Neale Hurston, *Mules and Men* (Philadelphia: Lippincott, 1935) have contributed most significantly to our knowledge of black folk culture. More recent works have continued to focus, in one way or another, on black creative art. Among the best are Daryl Cumber Dance, *Shuckin' and Jivin': Folklore from Contemporary Black Americans* (Bloomington: Indiana University Press, 1978); Roger D. Abrahams's *Deep Down in the Jungle: Negro Narrative Folklore from the Streets of Philadelphia* (Chicago: Aldine Publishing Co., 1963), his *Positively Black* (Englewood Cliffs, N.J.: Prentice-Hall, 1970), and his more recent *Afro-American Folktales* (New York: Pantheon Books, 1986). The introduction to the latter volume contains an excellent treatment of storytelling in black culture.

Although the primary focus of *Miles of Smiles* is not the storytelling process as such, there are several important works dealing with African and African-American tales and tale-telling that should be mentioned. Daniel Crowley, *I Could Talk Old-Story Good* (Berkeley: University of California Press, 1966) is an excellent examination of the art of storytelling in the Bahamas, while Peter Seitel, *See So That We May See* (Bloomington: Indiana University Press, 1980) is an important study of Haya folktales from a structuralist point of view. Other important studies include Daniel Crowley, ed., *African Folklore in the New World* (Austin: University of Texas Press, 1977); Michael J. Bell, *The World from Brown's Lounge: An Ethnography of Black Middle-Class Play* (Urbana: University of Illinois Press, 1983); and Norman E. Whitten, Jr., and John F. Szwed, eds., *Afro-American Anthropology: Contemporary Perspectives* (New York: The Free Press, 1970). An important and more recent work about black family stories and personal experience narratives is Kathryn Morgan, *Children of Strangers: The Stories of a Black Family* (Philadelphia: Temple University Press, 1980). Consistent with the Pullman porter narratives, and also with the slave narratives collected by the Works Progress Administration, the heroes of these personal narratives are real people who act as trickster figures. However, there has been little folkloristic work done with the Pullman porter. One notable exception is in the anthology *Mother Wit from the Laughing Barrel: Readings in the Interpretations of Afro-American Folklore*, Alan Dundes, ed. (Englewood Cliffs, N.J.: Prentice-Hall, 1973). In this volume, Dundes includes a short piece written by A. Philip Randolph, "The Human Hand Threat," originally published in *The Messenger* 4 (1922): 499–500, in which he discusses an instance of attempted intimidation through the manipulation of a Negro folk belief.

Among the many models for this study, Lawrence W. Levine's *Black Culture and Black Consciousness* is a historical study that works with expressive forms, both folk and popular, as cultural facts, as artistic entities that tell us about cultural perceptions both emic and etic, that is, from the insider's and the outsider's points of view. Folklorist Henry Glassie has long championed a unified theory of history and cultural studies; his *Passing the Time in Ballymenone* is exemplary in this regard. Of particular interest to me, and important to this study, is Barbara Myerhoff's *Number Our Days*. In that work, she also studied a group of elderly people who forged an identity together, in the here and now, based in large part on similar (if not shared) experiences they all had in the past. Moreover, Myerhoff's work also involved the making of a documentary film, entitled *Number Our Days*, just as the work that went into this study resulted in the ethnodocumentary film *Miles of Smiles, Years of Struggle: The Untold*

Story of the Black Pullman Porter. I found her methodological statements of particular relevance. For my part, I feel that the making of the film enriched my relationship with the porters involved, primarily because it necessitated that I enter into a contractual agreement with the film's principals. The result of this was a relationship of greater equality than I have otherwise experienced in the course of doing fieldwork. The porters were no longer "doing me a favor" by sitting down to an interview—they were as interested in seeing the film completed as I was—and I was no longer their "academic superior."

The work of other social scientists has informed this book a great deal. In addition to the many important works of Dell Hymes, I have been influenced by anthropologist Ralph Linton, particularly his description of "status" as a collection of rights and duties in The Study of Man (New York: D. Appleton-Century Co., Inc., 1936, 113) and by sociologist Erving Goffman's analysis of social behaviors as performance in The Presentation of Self in Everyday Life (Garden City, N.Y.: Doubleday Anchor Books, 1959). Raymond Williams's concepts of emergent and residual culture and of the interrelationship between the social base and cultural forms in his The Interpretation of Culture has also been relevant to this work, as has, in perhaps less obvious ways, the works of Clifford Geertz and Victor Turner. Turner's work on social dramas (Dramas, Fields, and Metaphors), for instance, underlies some of the ideas in this book. This concept is particularly relevant for workers in service occupations, such as porters, who themselves articulate concepts of being "onstage" and "backstage" as part of their work routines. See, for instance, Edward Swift and Charles Boyd, "A Pullman Porter Looks at Life," Psychoanalytical Review 15 (1928): 393–416. Historian Bernard Mergen has written of the usage of the appellation "George" in an article that has directed the attention of many of his colleagues, including myself, to the richness of the occupational history and culture of Pullman porters and their importance in American society. His article, "The Pullman Porter: From 'George' to Brotherhood," The South Atlantic Quarterly 74, 2 (1974), is perhaps the first real examination of porter culture in recent years and is an excellent exploration in general.

The field of occupational folklore is growing rapidly. A good introduction and overview of the concepts and approaches to occupational folklore and folklife is available in Robert H. Byington, ed., Working Americans (Washington, D.C.: Smithsonian Institution, 1978). Articles in that volume by Robert McCarl, Jr., Roger D. Abrahams, Robert H. Byington, and myself explore issues of definition, approach, fieldwork methodology, genre, and analysis. Archie Green's "Industrial Lore: A Bibliographic-Semantic Query" in that volume is a remarkable bibliographical essay on the development and notable achievements of researchers in this area of study. Much of the work in occupational culture has in the past dealt with the extractive industries, such as mining. George Korson's work in this area remains unsurpassed; see Angus K. Gillespie, Folklorist of the Coal Fields: George Korson's Life and Work (University Park: Pennsylvania State University

Press, 1980). Fishing has been well documented by Horace Beck in *Folklore and the Sea* (Brattleboro, Vt.: Stephen Greene, [1973] 1983), and in more recent studies such as Patrick B. Mullen, *I Heard the Old Fisherman Say: Folklore of the Texas Gulf Coast* (Austin: University of Texas Press, 1978). Robert McCarl's *The Washington, D.C. Firefighter Project* (Washington, D.C.: Smithsonian Institution, 1985) is a book-length study of urban firefighters, informed by months of on-site participatory fieldwork by the author. Richard M. Dorson's *Land of the Millrats* (Cambridge, Mass.: Harvard University Press, 1981) is a study of the urban area of Gary, Indiana.

Resources Relating to Pullman Porters

Brazeal, Harris, and Anderson each have done important studies on the founding and development of the BSCP. Primary resources include A. Philip Randolph's magazine, *The Messenger* (originally *The Hotel and Restaurant Messenger*), which was published from 1917 to 1928. It is a showcase for Randolph's thinking during those years and was also published during the period that the Union was founded. *The Pullman Porter*, a union pamphlet issued by the BSCP in New York in 1927, is a straightforward statement of the union's positions on such issues as the Employee Representation Plan. Another important "position paper" is C. F. Anderson, *Freemen Yet Slaves Under Abe Lincoln's Son, or, Service and Wages of Pullman Porters* (Chicago: S. C. White, 1904). The title refers to Robert T. Lincoln, who was indeed the son of the Great Emancipator, an irony that was not lost on the porters. W. H. Des Verney wrote an article, "Reminiscences of a Pullman Porter," in *The Pullman Porter's Review* 4, no. 1 (June, 1916), before he became a Brotherhood official in 1925, when the union was founded. Interestingly, fifteen years earlier, a small book entitled *Reminiscences of a Pullman Conductor*, by Herbert O. Holderness (Chicago, 1901), had included a highly sympathetic six-page chapter on porters. Although written in what was supposed to be dialect, the author called for better tips and even suggested a system of mandatory tips.

E. D. Nixon, of Montgomery, Alabama, has been interviewed on many occasions. Publications which include his recollections of the events leading to the Montgomery bus boycott include Studs Terkel, *Hard Times* (New York: Pantheon Press, 1970); Howell Raines, *My Soul Is Rested* (New York: G. P. Putnam's Sons, 1977); Milton Viorst, *Fire in the Streets* (New York: Simon and Schuster, 1979); and Martin Luther King, Jr., *Stride Toward Freedom: The Montgomery Story* (New York: Harper, 1958).

Pullman porters have been stereotyped in virtually all areas of popular culture. In nineteenth-century stage shows, black-face comedians did porter routines; cylinder discs and Edison recordings in the Library of Congress's Division of Recorded Sound contain some of this material. References to longer, plotted theatrical presentations such as "The Tourists in a Pullman Palace Car" can be found in works such as C. D. Odell, *Annals of the New York Stage* (New York: AMS Press, n.d.). This material appears similar to plots and skits that were used in later films. The Motion Picture Unit of the Library of Congress holds many early "paper prints" and early films referred to throughout this book. Literary works that feature Pullman porters, other than the works mentioned in chapter 5, include Preston Sturges, *Palm Beach Story*; James W. Johnson, *Autobiography of an Ex-Colored Man* (Boston: Sherman, French, and Co., 1912); Claude McKay, *Home to Harlem* (New York: Harper and Brothers, 1928); William Faulkner, *Sartoris* (New York: Harcourt, Brace, and Company, 1929), later restored and published in full as *Flags in the Dust* (New York: Random House, 1973). This is not intended as an exhaustive history of literary works, but rather an indication of some which feature porters as characters. An early short novel entitled *A Sleeping Car Porter's Experience, Treating in Brief Ordinary Life*, by C. Anderson (Chicago: n.d., but stamped 1916 by the Library of Congress) is an interesting work. Bernard Mergen has said that he finds the incidents described in *A Sleeping Car Porter's Experience* similar to the anecdotes I have described in this book and feels that the two works corroborate each other in this way.

Index